STARTING SOMEWHERE:
COMMUNITY ORGANIZING FOR SOCIALLY AWKWARD PEOPLE WHO'VE HAD ENOUGH

Roderick Douglass

With a foreword by Masai Andrews

Cover Sketch by Norman Losier
Cover Photography by Ashley Montalvo
Illustrations by Dominique Muñoz // @LSDomo

ISBN: 979-8-9918468-0-6

In memory of Nyah Mway

"The oppressor can never be trusted as historian. Our task is preservation. Collective memory is a liberation practice. Remember and tell it." — Cole Arthur Riley

CONTENTS

FOREWORD
BY MASAI ANDREWS

—July 11th, 2024

Two weeks ago, police in Utica, New York, shot and killed a 13-year-old boy. His name was Nyah.

Nyah had just graduated from middle school and was walking home from a graduation party on the night he was killed.

He and his friend were stopped by police for the crime of walking in the street, a violation of New York State Vehicle and Traffic Law 1156a. While frisking the boys, police asked if they had any weapons on them. Nyah took off running before being tackled, punched twice in the face, and then shot in the chest at point-blank range by officers. He died at the scene. Police later accused Nyah of having a BB gun in his possession.

I first learned of this incident from a frantic direct message I received from a woman living in Utica at the time. She was understandably distraught over the situation, and asked me what to do.

Over the years, I've received countless messages like this—a tragic incident of state violence occurs in a vulnerable community, prompting concerned organizers to reach out for guidance. Many of my comrades receive messages like this as well. I'm sure many of the people reading this do, too.

The murder of Nyah Mway was gut-wrenching, and because of his age in particular, I felt myself overcome with grief and rage. Despite this, the frantic messages I received following his death gave me hope.

Those reaching out for guidance are a reminder that people still care, and that we've not yet grown entirely desensitized or complacent to the never-ending onslaught of state violence and militarized aggression imposed on our communities.

I dread the day people stop reaching out for help in combating injustice, because that will be the day we've lost.

Still, it is my hope that communities everywhere develop the sustainable infrastructure necessary to take a more proactive approach to radical organizing, so we can prevent tragedies *before* they occur. It's far more difficult to learn the skills and techniques needed to keep our communities safe in the midst of chaos. So, rather than receive messages asking "Where do we start?" I hope to see more messages saying, "Join us in what we've already begun."

We must also keep in mind that the goal is not just to survive tragedies, but to thrive and progress culturally, socially, and politically. It is not enough to respond to high-profile injustices on a case-by-case basis, no matter how egregious they may be. Systemic oppression is a danger to us all.

For every Nyah Mway or Tamir Rice, thousands more children are being subjugated, neglected, and exploited every day under the countless systems working against us. For every Breonna Taylor or Sonya Massey, millions more adults are sacrificing their dreams, health, and lives slowly, over the course of decades, so that regressive institutions and oppressive governments can profit. And indeed, for every act of genocide in Palestine, there is also Haiti, Sudan, Syria, Yemen, The Congo, and more.

So where do we start?

Like most things, the answer isn't cut and dry. If you subscribe to the notion "Think globally, act locally," as I do, then half the question has been answered. We start where we live. It's not necessary to fly to D.C., or Flint, or Gaza to participate in the work of changing the world. We change the world by changing the world around us. The answers lie in our communities.

But there is no one-size-fits-all blueprint for community organizing. Effective organizing is imperfect and messy; and every group, neighborhood, and community must create a system that works for them. And those systems must constantly change and adapt over time in response to not only our circumstances, but to our resources, capacity, and readiness to intervene. Methods that work in one town are not guaranteed to work in another. Methods from yesterday are not promised to work tomorrow.

There should be a willingness to try new things and adopt established frameworks as needed. There should be an understanding that at times mistakes will be made and we will be wrong. And there should be an acceptance that at times we *must* make mistakes in order to move forward. As Malcolm X noted, "There is no better teacher than adversity. Every defeat, every heartbreak, every loss, contains its own seed, its own lesson on how to improve your performance the next time."

Please do not use this text as an authority or an excuse to limit courageous and untested means of resistance. Please do not use this text to evade accountability for your actions or inactions. After all, I'm just some guy. So was Malcolm. So was King. So was Marx. I'm not equating their virtues to my own; I'm equating our limitations and shortcomings. I'm equating our humanity.

Many of the things you will read in this text may not apply to you, but hopefully they will provide a reference or spark some ideas that will. So much of community organizing is simply having the courage to take the first step.

So when people ask me where to start, my go-to response is "Start somewhere."

I

OF PROMISES KEPT

I always said if I were to write a book I'd keep the first chapter extremely short.

THE HEIST
REFRAMING RESISTANCE

My first major arrest was for stealing loose change. Here's how it went:

I used to work as a front end supervisor at a local supermarket. A front end supervisor is a glorified cashier who gets paid $0.50 more an hour to tell other cashiers when to go on break. I had been working for this particular supermarket chain—Price Chopper—since high school, but had only recently been promoted.

During my short tenure as supervisor, management made the mistake of entrusting me with the key to their Coinstar machine—a kiosk at the front of the store that counts loose change and prints vouchers for the collective value, less a healthy "transaction fee." I was mainly supposed to fix printer jams or coin clogs from sticky pennies drenched in beer and ball sweat. The inner mechanism that counted change was essentially a rotating funnel with different-sized holes to sort various U.S. coins, as well as filter out debris and foreign currency. While working on the machines I quickly recognized a vulnerability.

My hack was simple:

I devised a secondary funnel out of plastic laminate to catch the coins and recirculate them back into the sorting mechanism—over and over again—artificially inflating the count.

"25 cents."
"50 cents."
"75 cents."
"One dollar."

The more coins I put in, the faster the voucher value would climb. I realized I could use dollar coins to speed things up.

"One dollar."
"Two dollars."
"Four dollars."
"Eight dollars."

So, late at night, I'd open the machine for "maintenance" and throw coins into my custom funnel. They'd circulate for a time, eventually resulting in a slip for a few hundred bucks. The whole process took minutes.

A co-worker and friend of mine—who would later become my co-defendant—cashed the first batch of slips at the customer service desk where we worked.

Obviously, when the coin company counted their change they'd recognize the discrepancy, but they only showed up every two weeks—long enough to significantly dilute the pool of suspects.

That first night we made $400. It would have been foolish to keep hitting the same machine, so we decided to take our show on the road.

Lucky for us, it turns out that if you walk into a random supermarket with a clipboard and a tie, nobody questions why you're messing with their coin machine. And we were surprised and delighted to find out the keys to all the machines were universal—a deficiency that has long since been addressed thanks to our shenanigans.

We wore ball caps and fake glasses to obscure our identity from security cameras and timed our trips during off-hours to catch the skeleton crew—staff who generally aren't too concerned with the goings-on of the store.

Then we'd start funneling dollar coins into our contraption until we had generated a high-value voucher. A few minutes later we were across the street at a competing supermarket cashing in the slips.

Often we'd pay someone outside to go in and cash the slips for us while we were inside rigging the next machine for a new batch of vouchers. Rinse and repeat. We did this for much of the summer. On a good weekend, we could hit three or four stores and make $1,600. As a result, we took a lot of road trips.

We eventually got caught the way all thieves get caught: We got cocky.

One weekend we decided enough time had passed to hit the first store again, back at Price Chopper. Unbeknownst to us, the coin company had been working with State law enforcement to track us down. They put cameras in several machines and waited months while we bounced around New York expanding our heist.

In retrospect, I'm glad we were caught before the Feds got involved, since our most recent excursions had taken us to supermarkets across state lines (which would have introduced a slew of new felonies). But it never got to that point.

One fateful day I walked in to work and the police were waiting for me along with the store manager. I left in handcuffs and spent the day in lock-up. My sister posted my bail with the mountain of cash back at my apartment.

Upon being released, I called my co-defendant who had already been informed by our co-workers of my arrest. He dressed comfortably the next day and was expectedly greeted by law enforcement at the start of his shift. He spent the night in jail and posted bail in similar fashion.

Coinstar wanted us to do serious time, but also didn't want the story to get too big because it made them look bad. Plus, if word got out before they'd addressed their deficiencies there would surely be copycats. To expedite our sentencing and reduce embarrassment, Coinstar decided to only press charges for the thefts at our initial workplace, which they could easily prove. We took the first plea deal that kept us out of prison and were sentenced to restitution and three years probation.

Thankfully, this was my first arrest and the judge assigned to our case found our crime entertaining, and said as much on a few occasions. We got off easy for what was clearly a string of brazen felonies. And best of all, our restitution was less than 1/4th of our cumulative haul for the summer. Needless to say, we paid in cash.

I later learned that Coinstar, along with Walmart, Price Chopper, Hannaford, and several other supermarket chains had to change their corporate policies and regulations nationwide because of our scam. Voucher slips now have strict value limits. The Coinstar machine itself was completely redesigned, and unique keys were made mandatory across the country. Coinstar staff also have to sign a logbook before providing maintenance to any machines in retail settings. This overhaul reportedly cost hundreds of thousands of dollars.

Today, I view this incident as my first successful direct action, but at the time I was embarrassed for getting arrested and losing my job. The shame and stigma of being labeled a criminal followed me for many years, until hindsight allowed me to look at the totality of circumstances.

For example, Coinstar—now a billion-dollar company—is legally allowed to take 12 cents for every dollar of currency they process. They're essentially trading cash for less cash, which is perfectly legal and even encouraged under capitalism. They've even won awards for finding innovative ways to rip consumers off. But there's no ethical way to make a billion dollars, ever, so the biggest crooks in my story were them.

Additionally, my heist didn't cause any communal harm. In fact, it helped pay my bills for the summer. It helped feed my friends and family. It helped fix my car. It even helped fund my ill-fated rap career—all while wasting the time and resources of the ruling class. Robbing Coinstar was more than a cash grab, it was an act of resistance. I'm a regular Robin Hood. Or at least, that's what I tell myself so I can keep telling this story at parties.

The point is: "Direct action gets the goods." In a class war between the Haves and the Have-nots, we're going to have to start reclaiming resources to get our point across. Even if it's just loose change.

I hope to encourage more individuals to reflect on any shame incurred while navigating oppression and reframe it as resistance personified. Challenging capitalism, white supremacy, patriarchy, homophobia, transphobia, ableism and everything in between is central to revolutionary work. And components of these systems take on many forms—from your shitty landlord, to your neglectful partner, to the author of this book, and likely the reader, too. But blame and shame alone do nothing to challenge institutional power.

True resistance requires education and action. It requires risk. And unfortunately, it requires sacrifice. But contrary to popular belief, crime often *does* pay, and swords can be mightier than pens—and not coincidentally, the people who say otherwise seem to own everything.

III

LOOK FOR THE HELPERS
FINDING OTHERS WHO THINK LIKE YOU

In the spring of 2018, I attended a lecture at SUNY Broome Community College given by Tarana Burke, founder of the #MeToo movement. She offered several profound insights on community organizing, but none stuck with me more than when she said, "Find five people who think like you, get in a room, and see what happens."

This is sage advice.

For all its complexities, building community is fundamentally about holding space with others while sharing ideas and resources. From the Irish Republican Army to the Wu-Tang Clan, successful anti-establishment movements across the globe have started with the simple premise of gathering in small groups. And as a result, those in power know there's no bigger threat to their current systems than oppressed people kickin' it. So kick it we must.

But when it comes to counterculture movements, especially within the confines of capitalism, finding people who are willing and able to meet can be challenging, if not outright dangerous. After all, the United States has literally passed laws to stop marginalized people from gathering in small groups.

"It shall not be lawful for more than five male slaves, either with or without passes, to assemble together at any place off the proper plantation to which they belong," reads the Alabama Slave Code of 1833.

Not coincidentally, Nat Turner, two years prior, shared his now-infamous rebellion plans with precisely four accomplices in whom "he had the greatest confidence." That rebellion resulted in the deaths of at least 55 white Southerners and inspired a new wave of rebels and abolitionists. But the consequences were staggering. Hundreds of Black folks were lynched following the uprising to send a message that resistance to slavery would not be tolerated. And that tradition of violently suppressing organized resistance continues to this day.

At a reproductive rights rally in Binghamton, New York, in the summer of 2022, a woman from the crowd commented that she'd driven three hours from her rural Pennsylvania town to attend. According to her, this was because it was physically unsafe for people in her area to gather publicly for progressive rallies and protests. Fortunately, this woman was able to use her privileges to gather with like-minded folks across state lines.

Indeed, I've known many commuter organizers over the years, who—for whatever reasons—were unwilling or unable to organize in their own communities. This can be beneficial for all parties involved: The commuters get to travel and organize in relative privacy and safety, and the cities they collaborate with get an outsider's perspective and resources to apply to their own organizing efforts. The main downsides are the time and costs associated with travel; and, of course, the nagging suspicion that the commuter must be an FBI informant. (They're probably not, but it won't hurt to vet them just to be on the safe side.)

For the vast majority, however, it's neither sustainable nor practical to organize far away from home, so advocates are left with two options: 1) Organize online, or 2) figure out how to organize locally, despite the challenges. Either way, the first step is finding others who share your commitment to liberation work. Below I'll outline some methods and strategies for connecting with people who think like you.

GO TO MEETINGS AND EVENTS
Hopefully this is obvious, but the absence of visible protests in your region doesn't necessarily mean there aren't other locals who share your ideals. Protests are tentpoles of movement work, but realistically they make up a tiny fraction of community organizing. People are working to improve the world around the clock. We just have to find them. To quote Mister Rogers, "Look for the helpers."

Are there mutual aid initiatives in your area? Who runs them? Who volunteers? Is there a local library? The goal is to interact with people so you can get a sense of where their politics lie. This can be difficult depending on where you live and what social disorders you have, but it's not impossible.

When I first moved to New York's Southern Tier, I attended every organizing meeting I could find. I also attended any event that seemed helpful to the community. I went to food pantries and offered to volunteer. I wasn't looking for these spaces in particular; I was looking for people who may know of more radical spaces that were less visible—and that's exactly what I was able to find after some digging.

It's impractical and redundant to create radical organizing spaces in communities where they already exist, so it makes more sense to find existing ones to lend a hand. But if you're convinced there are no Leftist spaces in your area, or if you simply don't feel in political alignment with them, only then should you endeavor to create new spaces from scratch.

START A BOOK CLUB, OR SOMETHING

Book clubs are a great way to find like-minded people, and you can do this both virtually and in person. You don't even have to read the book; just pick one that has a topic that potential comrades may be interested in. Don't start with *The Communist Manifesto*; try to be more subtle.

Make some flyers and hang them around town with an email address or a link to an online space. The goal is to catch the eye of folks who think like you. Don't like books? How about playing Spades? Roller-skating? Coffee? Feeding the hungry? Volunteering at an animal shelter? If you're Black or Indigenous, you probably already have people in your family who'd be down to gather periodically and conspire against the government. Ask around.

TALK TO YOUR NEIGHBORS

Striking up a conversation with a neighbor—Ya know what, never mind. I'm asking for too much. Moving on.

BE GAY, DO CRIME

Queer folks are experts at discreetly finding other queer people. The same is true of criminals and other societal outcasts. Fortunately, these groups are exactly who you want to be organizing with. Find them and make friends. Is there a skatepark in your town? An area that regularly has graffiti? A coffee shop with rainbow stickers in the window? Court is generally open to the public. Sit in on a few proceedings to find local troublemakers and their supporters.

The smaller the town, the harder you'll have to look. But it's generally easier to make a big impact in a small community since there's not much else happening. Plus, plenty of social misfits are low-key seeking camaraderie, even if we pretend we're not, so either way it's worthwhile.

SOCIAL MEDIA

At the time of this writing, social media is still a viable way to find like-minded people in your community, although I don't expect that to last much longer.

Algorithms and AI are making it harder and harder for radicals to occupy digital spaces unfettered. But for the time being, if you have access to Facebook you can search for social justice events that occurred in your area and try to connect with people who attended. Even a Black Lives Matter rally from years prior can help you identify left-leaning locals nearby. Find them, add them to your friends list, and try to make contact. If cops can use social media to locate people intent on toppling the government, so can you.

UNIONIZE YOUR CO-WORKERS

Work is a great place to organize people who share a common problem—exploitation. Put feelers out to see who wants a raise. Start talking openly about salaries and wages. Gather OUTSIDE of work to discuss other issues candidly. Network across departments and branches, if possible. Once you feel you have enough support, establish a formal committee and begin the process of unionizing. Generally, you only need 30% of employees on board at a worksite to start the process. That's doable. The hardest part is taking the first step.

But even if you don't manage to start a formal union, there are benefits to building alliances and solidarity with co-workers. Informal unions wield power and influence, too. Work stoppages, slowdowns, and mass sick-outs can all be coordinated if enough employees get on the same page. Don't let the absence of a formal union deter you from organizing among your peers.

SET A TRAP
Go to your local shopping plaza and tell the Customer Service Desk there's a Toyota Prius with a "Coexist" bumper sticker that's on fire. Wait for the announcement and then introduce yourself to everyone who runs outside. Thank me later.

~~~

Finding people who think like you doesn't mean participating in a hive-mind organization or working in a silo. It means finding those with a shared sense of compassion and empathy, along with a willingness to try and make the world a better place. Ideally, you want people involved with a diverse array of backgrounds and insights to bring to the table, so your plan of approach can be well-rounded and inclusive. The voices of the most marginalized should always be prioritized, because those are the groups with the most to lose and the clearest vantage point of systemic conditions.

Many Leftist organizers start in liberal spaces before transitioning to slightly more progressive groups (think "Democratic Socialists"), before ultimately moving to spaces that take a more radical approach to resistance. Rest assured, there are potential comrades out there actively searching for the right environment to allow them to advance politically and organizationally. If you feel like you're in a space that isn't challenging you to do better—or more importantly, challenging institutions of power—it may be time to expand your search and look elsewhere.

But never make the mistake of assuming you're alone. I guarantee there are people who know all too well that what is currently passing for society is a perverse and undignified affront to our existence. Look for the helpers, find them, and then find a path forward.

IV

PLANNED OBSOLESCENCE
THE ART OF DISPOSABLE ORGANIZING

In August of 2016, I attended the Second Continental Convening of Black Lives Matter in Greensboro, North Carolina. The convention was coordinated by the national organization, but open to regional chapters. It occurred at the height of the Black Lives Matter movement, which had been propelled into overdrive in response to a wave of high-profile incidents of police violence, as well as the frightening prospect of Trump's first presidency.

The four-day convening took place at the luxurious Marriott Hotel in downtown Greensboro, and was attended by roughly 300 Black organizers from all over the country. The gorgeous hotel suites—75 in total— were booked and paid for by the Black Lives Matter Global Network, at no cost to us. I never did the math at the time, but I calculate the rooms alone cost upwards of $50,000. And that doesn't include the money spent on food, airfare, speaking fees, and swag.

During the conference, I networked with organizers I knew from social media—many of whom I still have relationships with today. I met Samaria Rice, mother of Tamir Rice, who had been killed by police less than two years prior. I spoke with Pasadena organizer Jasmine Richards, who had famously served 90 days in jail for "felony lynching" after attempting to physically remove a Black woman from police custody. I sat in on a lecture given by Professor Melina Abdullah—a co-founder of BLM Los Angeles whose work I admired. I attended workshops on security protocols, base building, and direct action; and I got ridiculously drunk every single night, with as many people as possible.

I admit, I was impressed by the atmosphere and the allure of enjoying a few days of relative luxury among so many radical folks. But the whole thing felt a bit "off."

Tensions were high as torrents of emotion coursed through the halls of the hotel. The accommodations could only temporarily mask the undertones of grief and frustration that stood in stark contrast to the swanky venue. Gradually, things began to unravel. On the third day, there was a presentation called "Where Do We Go From Here?" which featured limited information on the organization's finances. This was the final straw.

Until that point, many of us in attendance had no idea how much money was being donated to the BLM Global Network. We're still not 100% sure, but it was a lot. And it helped explain how and why the org was willing to splurge so extravagantly on the convening. Regional chapters were organizing tirelessly under the BLM banner, and those efforts had essentially become a non-stop fundraiser for the national organization. Millions of dollars in donations and grants were lining the BLM Network's coffers, while individual chapters and organizers were resorting to GoFundMe campaigns just to keep the lights on. The presentation devolved into chaos and never regained composure. The convening ended on the sourest of notes, and we all headed back home to report what we'd learned.

Many chapters dissolved that night. Others rebranded over time. A few stayed on board in an attempt to access some of the funding. My chapter, BLM Upstate New York, had several discussions and eventually decided to intentionally and methodically transition out of the BLM Global Network, which we viewed as a sinking ship. I drafted a document entitled "10 Steps to Transitioning BLM Upstate NY," which was basically a plan for shedding the BLM name while maintaining the infrastructure we'd built over the years. We never got to implement this plan, as the chapter eventually collapsed on its own, but we all saw the writing on the wall well in advance. For all its talk of grassroots radical organizing, BLM Global was being run like a business, and that was a serious problem. At least to us.

Businesses are designed to grow exponentially as stipulated by capitalism, presumably with the ultimate goal of world domination. In hindsight, the name "BLM

Global Network" should have been a red flag. Global organizations aren't practical, manageable, or sustainable in an anti-capitalist context. It is corporations and governments that seek to expand indefinitely.

The Pepsi Company, for example, doesn't have a maximum profit threshold where they would stop selling soda. If it were left to them, they'd grow forever until every dollar in the world was in their possession. The same can be said of "nonprofits" like The Red Cross ($4.03B total assets, 2023) and the United Way ($3.5B total revenue, 2023). In fact, as noted in *The Revolution Will Not Be Funded: Beyond the Non-Profit Industrial Complex*, the US nonprofit sector is "a trillion-dollar industry" and "one of the world's largest economies."

Anti-capitalist organizations, however, should not be run like businesses, and should arguably dismantle and dissolve every few years as they continue to adapt to meet the needs of The People™. If an organization prioritizes its own financial viability and longevity over the sustainability of the community it purports to serve, that organization is, by definition, capitalist.

Think of radical community organizations as the scaffolding used to repair and maintain large buildings representing local communities.

The goal is for a given community to flourish, INDEPENDENT of any singular organization or network. It doesn't matter if the organization fails, just like it doesn't matter if the scaffolding collapses—because the building remains.

What usually ends up happening is a group fades into obscurity—or worse—gets infiltrated and/or implodes due to mismanagement, conflict, or becoming a target for law enforcement. Media narratives also start to vilify radical orgs, which can ultimately dilute the work and create a culture of "damage control" and defensiveness. This happened to the Black Panthers; it happened to the Student Nonviolent Coordinating Committee (SNCC); it's still happening to BLM chapters, and is arguably also happening to "Antifa," which mainly exists in the minds of conservatives.

All of this can be avoided if the branding and structure of a movement are disposable, ever-changing, and secondary to the work being done.

The measure of an effective organization isn't in how long it lasts, it's how the community endures once it inevitably fails. "The Revolutionary is a doomed man," according to radicals like Sergey Nechayev. The system will eventually do what it must to protect itself—either by wearing us down, co-opting our efforts, tossing us in prison, or outright ending our lives.

There's a reason the NAACP still exists but the much more radical MOVE organization in Philadelphia had a bomb dropped on their headquarters by the U.S. government.

It's rare to encounter orgs or individuals who've been effectively fighting the system for decades on end, unless they've stopped challenging institutional power in any significant sense. Career activists are just that. Radicals are not seeking long-term employment, but transformative change.

Fortunately, as Fred Hampton noted, "You can kill a revolutionary, but you can never kill the Revolution."

Does that mean radicals and revolutionaries are all sacrificial lambs awaiting an inevitable slaughter? No. Revolutionaries who manage to survive can and should master the art of passing the torch whilst picking up a new one. And as long as human societies exist there will always be liberation work for us to engage in. Being disposable does not mean our value expires over time. As I mentioned before, prisons are filled with freedom fighters (I may even be one of them by the time you read this), and for many their work continues even after being incarcerated. Let their sacrifice be an inspiration, not the goal. Or, as Abbie Hoffman reflected in his seminal work, *Steal This Book*:

> Don't get hung up on a sacrifice trip.
> Revolution is not about suicide, it is about
> life. With your fingers probe the holiness
> of your body and see that it was meant to
> live. Your body is just one in a mass of cuddly
> humanity. Become an internationalist and learn
> to respect all life. Make war on machines, and
> in particular the sterile machines of corporate

death and the robots that guard them. The duty of a revolutionary is to make love and that means staying alive and free. That doesn't allow for cop-outs. Smoking dope and hanging up Che's picture is no more a commitment than drinking milk and collecting postage stamps. A revolution in consciousness is an empty high without a revolution in the distribution of power.

So take pride in your organizing efforts. Do good work. Print some t-shirts. Break the law. Then transition before you become big enough to fail. Our loyalty and commitment should be to The People™, not some logo. Not some brand. Not some organization.

If done correctly, the networks forged will remain intact long after we've departed, and our communities will persevere.

V

SANKOFA
LESSONS FROM THE 2020 UPRISINGS

On September 4th, 2020, I was arrested in Rochester, New York and charged with rioting. I was there to participate in a demonstration in response to the murder of Daniel Prude, a disabled Black man who was horrifically killed by police in early Spring. Prude's death occurred a few days after Breonna Taylor's and a few weeks before George Floyd's, so the country was already on edge. Rochester police intentionally delayed the release of bodycam footage depicting Prude's arrest in an attempt to prevent riots.

"I'm wondering if we shouldn't hold back on this for a little while considering what is going on around the country," one RPD Lieutenant wrote in an email to Rochester's then-Chief, La'Ron Singletary. But by the time the footage came out, tensions had only worsened. Additionally, the circumstances of Prude's murder were exceedingly egregious, even compared to other police killings of that year.

On March 23rd, 2020, Daniel Prude was in the midst of a mental health crisis. His brother called emergency services for help. When police arrived around 3 a.m., Prude was walking the streets naked and bleeding in the freezing cold. Prude complied with police orders to get on the ground and put his hands behind his back, and was quickly placed in handcuffs. But the frozen pavement on his bare skin caused him to go into further distress. He began spitting and cursing in response to the pain.

To remedy this, police put a white bag called a "spit hood" over Prude's head, but failed to cover his exposed and trembling body. The hood made it difficult for Prude to breathe, which caused him to become even more distressed. In response, three officers piled on top of him, pinning him to the frigid pavement and further obstructing his airway. Prude later died of complications from asphyxia. He was smothered to death.

When the video footage was finally released in early September, it immediately prompted a national outcry. Organizers and activists from all over the Northeast descended on Rochester to aid in mobilization efforts. I arrived along with a team of seasoned organizers on the third night of protests to provide tactical and medical support.

Although I had been arrested a half dozen times before for various acts of civil disobedience, to date, my arrest in Rochester remains the most traumatic and violent encounter I've ever had with law enforcement.

That night, a crowd of roughly a thousand rallied and marched for hours before arriving at the Court Street bridge on our way to Rochester Police headquarters.

Some of the participants were wearing helmets and protective gear after earlier demonstrations were met with overwhelming police force. Most of us, however, had no protection outside of perhaps a few umbrellas and surgical masks.

I was near the front of the line pulling a wagon full of water and medical supplies as we approached the bridge. Police opened fire on the crowd without warning and pummeled us with pepper balls and tear gas. Pepper balls are acorn-sized munitions meant to be fired at solid surfaces causing the balls to burst and release a cloud of pepper irritant into the air. That night, police were using pepper balls to fire directly into the crowd, hitting many participants in the face and head. The previous night police had used the same tactic, leaving one man permanently blind.

I was shot more than a dozen times, all over my arms, legs, and torso. The rounds hit with such velocity that I was covered in welts and bruises over most of my body. The pepper burned our eyes and made breathing extremely difficult. The crowd fell back and began to fortify the front lines with shields made from plywood, umbrellas, garbage can lids, and anything that could be used to deflect the onslaught of police rounds. Police would later accuse participants of throwing water bottles before they opened fire, but I know for a fact that didn't happen as I was right at the front.

I attempted, for a time, to keep people organized and calm to prevent a stampede. I knew from prior experience that we were safer together, and that our numbers were still ample enough to regroup and hold our ground. Someone tossed me a bullhorn, and I began rallying people to stay close and not scatter. I told the crowd that we'd have to prepare to protect ourselves once police started making arrests. Many in the crowd were receptive to my words, which prompted police to shoot me in the back with another round of pepper balls. At one point I put my hands in the air in a desperate attempt to de-escalate the situation and stop getting shot. Police took the opportunity to rush towards me and tackle me to the ground.

I was the first person taken into custody that night.

00844_AB2182
2020/09/04 23:31:54

Me, moments before being arrested in Rochester, New York

For what it's worth, none of us were "rioting." None of us were throwing bottles—although we would have been justified in doing so. We were on the front lines attempting to keep people safe. We were using our bodies to shield vulnerable people from the onslaught of munitions being launched into the crowd. Some of us were visibly bleeding while being taken into custody.

Myself and three others arrested shortly after me were locked in the cargo bay of a police van, no larger than a storage closet, that quickly filled with the pepper spray coating our clothing and bodies. For about a half hour we coughed violently while struggling to breathe. We pleaded for the officers to open a window or detain us outside. They laughed. One detainee lost consciousness briefly. Another vomited. None of us received medical attention.

Two separate officers—one Black and one white— verbally threatened to uncuff me and beat me upon my release. A young, white college student detained alongside me couldn't believe what he was hearing. We were transported to an isolated parking lot across town and put in a large sheriff's vehicle that looked like an old school bus. There we were screamed at and threatened some more. An officer joked he would purposely lose my personal items because I "had a big mouth." For the rest of the night he called me "fat fuck" and "doughboy."

The three individuals I was arrested with were all men. One guy was around my age and told me the police knocked him off his bicycle before taking him into custody. Two younger men were on opposite ends of the economic spectrum: There was the aforementioned college student participating in his very first protest, and a Black homeless kid.

After about 20 minutes on the sheriff's bus (not sure why they held us there) we were all placed back into the small, pepper-filled van and taken to the police station. They let us out of the vehicle and began processing us near a holding pen just outside the barracks. The holding pen had a handful of other detainees who were presumably arrested sometime after my group.

A sergeant on the scene was verbally abusive to all of us. He was angry that protestors had apparently started setting off fireworks after the first wave of arrests. I said "Good" when I heard this news, and he grabbed me and tossed me back in the pepper-filled van as punishment. I sat there alone for about 15 minutes fighting to breathe.

Eventually I was moved to the outdoor holding pen with a dozen others. I immediately noticed that one of the detainees was in a wheelchair. His name was Chris. He was reportedly arrested while attempting to use his chair to shield another protester lying on the ground. Police begrudgingly released him after someone in charge said it "looked bad" to keep him in custody. Chris wished us all good luck as police rolled his chair into the street in the dead of night without so much as an explanation.

The remaining detainees and I began talking amongst ourselves. I learned that another protester was shot in the eye during the stand-off and treated by street medics on the scene. I learned that police beat people with shields and batons to clear the Court Street bridge. I learned that many in the crowd were injured while running for their lives. Apparently, we were lucky to have been arrested early on, as police significantly escalated their attack once the first group of arrestees was in custody.

As we talked, time crawled forward. Police kept us standing outside in the holding pen for about three hours. Our hands were cuffed behind our backs the entire time, and large welts had developed on our wrists. Numbness and agony set in and our shoulders burned from being contorted for so long. I would have done anything to regain circulation to my arms. Eventually, cramping set in due to dehydration. Most of us were still covered in pepper spray and hadn't been given so much as a glass of water, let alone an eye rinse.

And then it was over.

I was driven to a bus station around 4 a.m. and released with an appearance ticket charging me with rioting and disorderly conduct. A year later, a judge dropped all the charges, but the abuse I endured that night radicalized me more than anything else I'd experienced at the time. I sustained nerve damage to my right hand from being in handcuffs for over four hours. It took me about nine months to regain full sensation in all my fingers. It's fair to say I hated police before the summer of 2020, but afterward I had a deeper appreciation of the danger that fascism posed to us all.

And I wasn't alone.

The social uprisings in the spring and summer of 2020 constituted the largest sustained mass mobilization to ever occur on American soil, with over 20 million participants nationwide. From late May through October, demonstrators took to the streets in numbers America had never before seen. More than 14,000 participants were arrested in the first month alone. The mass arrests overwhelmed the courts. According to *The Guardian*, "The vast majority of citations and charges against [2020] protesters were ultimately dropped, dismissed or otherwise not filed."

In many ways, these demonstrations were the culmination of the Black Lives Matter movement and the anti-Trump movement—in their 7th and 4th years, respectively. This is significant if we hope to understand the circumstances that made these uprisings possible.

And while American unrest had been building for years and even decades prior to 2020, one could reasonably argue that these uprisings had two major catalysts: 1) The economic collapse spurred by the coronavirus pandemic, and 2) The heinous police killings of Breonna Taylor and George Floyd in the spring of that year.

The combination of stay-at-home orders, record-setting unemployment, and righteous outrage from racialized police violence proved to be the perfect recipe for rebellion. Americans who may have normally opted out of the discussion or ignored the circumstances altogether were suddenly given both the time to assess—and the will to participate—in social movements. And all of this occurred despite public health restrictions that discouraged and (once again) criminalized socializing.

The wave of unrest felt unstoppable, and there was a collective realization of how fragile and volatile society had become. Every night you could turn on the news and see a different business or police station in flames. The unemployment rate peaked at staggering levels not seen since the Great Depression. I don't think it's an overstatement to say the United States was on the brink of social collapse.

In an effort to calm the unrest and uncertainty, massive social programs were implemented, seemingly overnight. Nearly all Americans received stimulus checks to help cover bills and infuse the economy. Unemployment insurance and food stamp benefits were maxed out for individuals and families across the board. Eviction moratoriums were put in place to stop landlords from evicting tenants who could no longer pay rent. Student loans and mortgage payments were put on hold for months and years at a time. And a child tax credit was implemented: giving parents an additional $250 to $300 per child, per month, for two full years.

All of this was happening against the backdrop of the impending 2020 Presidential race between Donald Trump (R) and Joe Biden (D). That the election even took place was remarkable, considering the complete disarray and chaos occurring in the months prior. But the election did occur, and it yielded the highest voter turnout for any national election in more than 100 years. Americans were desperate for change, and voting provided an outlet that was more palatable than total civil upheaval.

For better or worse, tempers cooled following Joe Biden's victory at the polls, and revolutionary work entered a new cycle. Abolitionist George Jackson highlighted this cyclical nature of revolution a few decades prior in his 1971 interview with Karen Wald:

> Right now, we are in a peak cycle. There's tremendous energy out there, directed against the state. It's not all focused, but it's there, and it's building. Maybe this will be sufficient to accomplish what we must accomplish over the fairly short run. We'll see, and we can certainly hope that this is the case. But perhaps not. We must be prepared to wage a long struggle. If this is the case then we'll probably see a different cycle, one in which the revolutionary energy of the people seems to have dispersed, run out of steam. But – and this is important – such cycles are deceptive. Things appear to be at low ebb, but actually what's happening is a period of regroupment, a period in which we

step back and learn from the mistakes made during the preceding cycle.

And step back we did. There was a massive shift to "get back to work" following the 2020 election, and many of the social protections implemented during the early months of COVID were gradually phased out.

But during those months of record-breaking unrest, a transformation took place that resulted in not just legislative advancements and appeasement, but social and cultural changes to the way communities approached organizing and mutual aid. Americans got a taste of stability from shared wealth, housing protections, and broadscale social programs, and many were reluctant to go back.

From the ashes of chaos came hope and progress, and a glimpse of how socialism could help America's most vulnerable. The tragic circumstances of a global pandemic, combined with a wave of police violence, resulted in a massive and rapid shift towards social progress.

As noted by Vladimir Lenin, "There are decades where nothing happens; and there are weeks where decades happen." Decades certainly happened in the spring and summer of 2020.

And we've seen this pattern over and over again.

For example, the Abolitionist Movement to end slavery in the United States abruptly shifted after the Civil War with the passing of the 15th Amendment in 1870, which theoretically granted Black men the right to vote. This helped expand the Women's Suffrage Movement, which responded the following year by sending "a voting rights petition to the Senate and House of Representatives requesting that [voting] rights be extended to women."

But nothing happened. The movement stalled. The cycle appeared to be at a "low ebb" for nearly *five decades* until tragedy kicked things into overdrive.

According to Stanford legal scholar Pamela Karlan, it took the turmoil of World War I—combined with the raging Spanish Flu pandemic—to "change the dynamic and ultimately strengthen the suffrage movement."

By 1918, President Woodrow Wilson, who had previously dismissed the movement, declared the voting rights of women a "vitally necessary war measure" that would help prove that the Allied Powers were indeed fighting for democracy. Additionally, as noted by *New York Times* journalist Alisha Gupta, "The [Spanish] flu would end up helping the suffragists' cause," which ultimately paved the way for "women's right to vote."

The domestic and medical demands of the pandemic combined with the industrial demands of World War I gave women increased power and visibility that could no longer be ignored. This increase in social capital bolstered feminist movements and led to the speedy passage of the 19th Amendment, affording white women the right to vote. Society took a little victory lap, and the ensuing wave of progress (now known as the Progressive Era) helped usher in new cultural and social movements—from the overall expansion of labor rights to the Harlem Renaissance.

And Americans lived happily ever after. Oh, wait, no—tragedy struck yet again. The Great Depression hit in 1929, and American society nearly collapsed, leading to another wave of massive uprisings.

In his 1935 best-selling novel, *It Can't Happen Here*, political author Sinclair Lewis famously dramatized the widely-held belief that America was on the brink of revolution during the Depression. It was this ever-present threat of revolution that forced President Franklin Roosevelt to implement the sweeping New Deal social initiatives that ironically prompted detractors to label him a "socialist" and a "communist."

FDR's social initiatives, however—along with the onset of a second World War—eventually helped save the US economy, allowing the country to compose itself. But once again, that would not have been possible without women and other oppressed groups filling critical societal roles while white men were off fighting. These cultural shifts helped spark the modern Civil Rights Movement of the 1950s and '60s.

And guess what: The Civil Rights Movement came to a bittersweet end as well with the murder of Martin Luther King—which led to massive riots—and the swift passing of the Civil Rights Act of 1968 in order to stop those riots. Prior to King's murder, fair housing legislation had completely stalled in Congress. It wasn't until people in more than 100 cities started burning down buildings and causing millions of dollars in property damage that the bill was expeditiously passed and signed into law—only two days after King's funeral.

Hopefully, you're noticing a trend.

"Bad things" (war, pandemics, riots) go hand in hand with "good things" (social advancement, progressive legislation, human rights). And societal changes are often imposed swiftly following chaos to prevent the pendulum from swinging too far and toppling the nation. **Progressive gains are accompanied by significant losses because social progress inherently requires sacrifice.**

Times of tragedy force society to deviate from social norms in the interest of self-preservation, causing citizens to question the merit of those norms. And the threat of revolution can persuade those in power to offer significant concessions to prevent societal collapse.

Often, American uprisings are prompted by regressive and violent institutions attempting to assert or reassert their power—from global warfare, to the queerphobic police raids on the Stonewall Inn, to the racist War on

Drugs. But occasionally, it would seem, this social push-back can be aided by a global pandemic or two [Editor's Note: This is merely an observation, not a call for more plagues].

Regardless, there are lessons to be learned from the 2020 Uprisings, and those in power are already busily re-writing history in the hopes we'll forget how close we came to toppling their empire. It's important we don't let that happen.

VI

TRASH TALK
DETERMINING THE NEEDS OF YOUR COMMUNITY

The Young Lords were a street-level organization founded by Puerto Rican activist Cha Cha Jiménez that operated from the late 1960s through the late 1970s. They are often described as the Puerto Rican answer to the Black Panther Party, which was highly visible and influential during the same period. Jiménez organized the Young Lords to combat racism and police brutality in Puerto Rican neighborhoods throughout Chicago, but chapters quickly popped up in major cities across the nation. The New York chapters in Harlem and the South Bronx raised the organization's profile and became central to their work and legacy.

The Young Lords and the Black Panthers shared a common ideology, and the groups would occasionally collaborate to enhance their overlapping agendas. Notably, the Young Lords wore purple berets to distinguish themselves from the Panthers' iconic black. The Young Lords were also vocally and critically supportive of women's rights and LGBT rights, and encouraged a diverse membership and base.

When the first chapters in New York were formed, the founders promptly set out to establish and define their local agendas. They did so by canvassing neighborhoods and asking residents directly what their biggest concerns were in the city. The answer they received, as recalled by Chairman Felipe Luciano in the 1996 documentary *¡Palante Siempre Palante!*, was surprising:

"So we're on 110th Street and we actually asked the people, 'What do you think you need? Is it housing? Is it [ending] police brutality?'" Luciano says. "And they said, 'Muchacho, déjate de todo eso—LA BASURA!' [Listen kid, fuggedaboutit! It's THE GARBAGE!] And I thought, my God, all this romance, all this ideology, to pick up the garbage?"

To say the 40-square-block area of Harlem where Luciano and the Young Lords were canvassing had a serious trash problem would be an understatement. The neighborhood was neglected and under-served by the city, and garbage was piled up along every curb. This led to health issues, unfathomable odors, and a rat infestation of epidemic proportions.

To address this issue, the Lords stole brooms from the NYC sanitation department and started sweeping the trash into major intersections where it couldn't be ignored by the city. When buses and commuter traffic started driving over the trash, the Lords fortified the mounds with furniture, sinks, and mattresses to make them harder to bypass. For extra effect, they'd often light these piles of trash on fire, forcing police and fire departments to be dispatched to the area. "The Garbage Offensive," as it came to be called, essentially made Harlem's trash problem EVERYONE'S trash problem, which pushed the city to divert additional resources into sanitation services for the neighborhood.

The Garbage Offensive of 1969

Although tackling trash wasn't initially on the Young Lords' radar, the garbage problem in Harlem stemmed from the same systemic inequalities and racial injustices they'd originally set out to combat. Neighborhoods with majority Black and brown residents are less likely to receive the services and resources necessary to function safely and efficiently; while rich, white neighborhoods are often the ones best serviced and maintained. Anyone who lives in a city where snow has to be plowed already knows this. But without creating a dialogue with local residents to discuss their issues and brainstorm solutions, The Garbage Offensive may never have taken place.

When organizing radically in a given community, one of the critical steps is determining what we hope to accomplish—both as organizations and individuals. Generally speaking, radical community groups fall into two distinct yet overlapping categories: **social justice orgs** and **charity orgs**. Social justice orgs focus on combating the root causes of oppression and finding sustainable solutions, while charity orgs focus on lessening the symptoms of oppression.

Ideally, you'd have an intentional mix of both in your organizational framework—sometimes collectively referred to as *mutual aid.* This is because charity is a constant, never-ending endeavor that can cause more harm than good by inadvertently masking the symptoms of oppression and therefore sustaining capitalism— and that's the best-case scenario. Charity's worst-case scenario is dedicating all of our collective time and resources towards treating the symptoms of oppression without making a dent towards addressing the immediate needs of The People™.

Imagine if all tent cities and homeless encampments disappeared overnight, and all the inhabitants were taken in by the church (charity). That would essentially "invisablize" the systemic problem of homelessness, without addressing the need for universal housing (justice). Jails and prisons consistently house more people than the church in any given year, but that doesn't make them good for society, either. Concealing problems can exacerbate them by removing systemic issues from public consciousness. Does that mean churches should shut their doors to the poor? No. It means we must prioritize ending homelessness over simply providing charity and temporary reprieve. The same is true of all social problems.

Finding the right balance of charity and justice can be challenging. It's easy to get overwhelmed by the sheer amount of immediate need in marginalized communities, but finding ways to empower people while also working towards ending systemic injustice is the only viable path forward.

Like non-profits, charity-based service orgs run the risk of co-opting movement work and diverting valuable energy and resources away from radical, sustainable initiatives. Soup kitchens are not the answer to hunger; food equity is. Shelters and jails are not the answer to homelessness, universal housing is. And "harm reduction," as it pertains to social justice, is a double-edged sword that must be wielded carefully. If we focused primarily on charity work it would be impossible to liberate communities and end suffering.

That being said, heed the words of civil rights leader Cesar Chavez, "The people who give you their food, give you their heart."

Feed those who are hungry. Find ways to clothe and house the needy. Share medicine with the sick. Sweep up trash if necessary. Charity is not a zero-sum game. But remember, the goal is to eventually make charity obsolete through social revolution. Community organizing is a tool we use to ensure that happens.

Generally, orgs tend to adapt to the given needs of a community based on ever-changing social conditions and current events. Since all social issues are interrelated under capitalism, it can make sense for anti-capitalist organizations to avoid limiting themselves to a singular initiative—especially in smaller communities lacking resources and volunteers. But often communities rally around one glaring injustice before branching out to broader underlying issues.

The Young Lords didn't plan on spearheading a trash rebellion, but because that was the dominant issue in their neighborhood, they took up that mantle early on. Similarly, the Black Panthers never intended their Free Breakfast Program to be a cornerstone of their work, but the needs of Black communities guided their efforts.

"Any program that's brought into our community," wrote Black Panther chairman Fred Hampton, "should be analyzed by the people of that community. It should be analyzed to see that it meets the relevant needs of that community." This tradition carried over into the Black Lives Matter movement, which originally focused on criminal justice reforms and ending police violence before establishing local agendas covering everything from clean water initiatives to housing justice.

If your community organization already has an agreed-upon focus that's relevant to your community, go ahead and flesh out your mission statement and get to work. Just remember, the goal is to be fluid and disposable. It's absolutely fine if you start out to tackle food insecurity and then pivot to trans rights. All suffering is interrelated. What's important is that there are mechanisms in place to combat injustice.

If you don't know exactly where to direct your energy, you're gonna wanna sort that out ASAP. The best way to do that is through outreach and talking to the most marginalized people in your community—which may very well include you. We don't simply advocate *for* people. We *are* The People™. So whether this involves going door-to-door, hosting a Town Hall, or simply talking to your neighbors about the trash, determine the community's needs and let them guide your organizing efforts.

One last suggestion: If you do go door-to-door in low-income neighborhoods, try not to carry clipboards or physically knock on doors, as both can be off-putting to residents. You're better off verbally announcing yourself (try "Hellooooo!" or "Yerrrrrr!") and taking notes on your phone. Trust me on this one. Good luck.

VII

MEET & GREET
SORRY, WE NEED TO HAVE MEETINGS

One Tuesday evening, I was eating dinner with my kids at our local Denny's. I know it was Tuesday because that's the day kids eat free, and I'm cheap.

This particular dinner was fairly unremarkable until we heard a jingle at the main entrance and looked up to see a large party entering the restaurant, consisting of about 20 adults of all genders, shapes, and sizes. Many were clad in fishnets and black leather. Some were older individuals with long biker beards, yet wearing frills and makeup. Others had heavy eyeliner and tattoos, and a few looked completely "normal," for lack of a better word—like they could have been soccer moms and accountants.

The woman who appeared to be their leader bypassed the hostess entirely and quickly ushered her motley crew to a private dining area in the rear of the restaurant— presumably where they hold birthday parties and the like.

But these guests seemed too comfortable and familiar with the routine for this to be a birthday dinner.

Once inside the space, the leader hopped on a chair and pulled down a large privacy shade to conceal the room from the front of the restaurant. A waitress hurriedly followed them inside with a notepad in hand and shut the door behind her. I remember thinking to myself, "I hope this is some sort of sex cult," before continuing to finish my Moons Over My Hammy®.

I later learned that what I had witnessed is referred to as a *munch* in the BDSM community. [Editor's Note: This is not to be confused with the AAVE term "munch," popularized by rapper Ice Spice, which refers to a sexual partner—typically a man—used almost exclusively for eating pussy.] A munch, according to kink and culture writer David Shorb, is a casual social gathering for people involved in kink, BDSM and/or fetish play, although no "play" activities actually take place during the gathering. "It's a time to just be social and talk to your fellow kinksters," writes Shorb. "It's a way to make connections and to get involved in your local community."

At the time, however, I knew none of this and only made a mental note that Denny's had a private backroom that could be reserved for community meetings. Fast forward six months, and I found myself packed into that same private room, along with two dozen other communists, for a meeting of our own.

Like protests and mutual aid, community meetings are cornerstones of revolutionary work. We can't have a successful Revolution without meetings, and that's the most depressing thing you will read in this book. The good news, however, is that the meetings we've grown accustomed to in Western society are a byproduct of white supremacy, and not in any way indicative of how meetings should be (or have historically been) conducted in communal spaces.

For generations, the Haudenosaunee (Iroquois) nations of what is today Upstate New York held private political meetings in the longhouses that also served as their homes. These gatherings were typically structured around a meal and may incorporate pipe smoking, drinking, and/or drumming throughout. Participants included a council of elders, chiefs, clan mothers, and faith keepers. Issues would be debated among these leaders and groups before arriving at a decision, which would then be announced to an open council consisting of broader members of the various nations. These meetings were formal, but not rigid or impersonal since they were held in domiciles and among family.

Centuries later, meetings held by the Student Non-Violent Coordinating Committee (SNCC)—which grew out of the sit-ins of the 1960s—were arguably more structured, but they still deviated from Western norms in a variety of ways. For example, it wasn't uncommon for SNCC meetings to go on for several days at a time, prioritizing meticulous clarity and exhaustive deliberation over speed in decision-making. Unburdened by the capitalistic expectation that issues be resolved overnight, SNCC would discuss issues at length with the ultimate goal of a consensus rather than a simple majority vote. SNCC meetings weren't just spaces for strategizing; they were platforms for dissent and political education through debate and dialogue.

As noted by author and national security advisor Thomas Ricks, "Leaders and staff members of the civil rights movement prepared well for meetings, took those sessions seriously, and used them to develop action plans they could implement. Movement leaders used meetings to explore their differences in agonizing detail. They did this because it was a movement maxim that if you were asking people to put their lives on the line—and they were—then it was essential to hear out their concerns."

The takeaway here is that meetings are important, but it's equally important that we don't conduct them under capitalist frameworks when organizing to subvert capitalism. Or as Audre Lorde so succinctly put it, "The master's tools will never dismantle the master's house." Community meetings shouldn't feel like we're at work, even when work is being done.

I pride myself on my approach to coordinating community meetings, but full disclosure: My approach is almost entirely drawn from things I learned during my years as an underground rapper. So as with everything in this book, take it with a salt enema. But underground rap shows and community meetings have two notable things in common: 1) Nobody wants to attend, and 2) Nobody wants to stay for long. So it's our job as organizers to overcome these challenges.

Below are some techniques to employ when throwing a radical grassroots community meeting:

FIND AN ACCESSIBLE SPACE

Thanks to the ongoing landlord crisis, finding a building to host organizational meetings can often be the hardest part. Depending on the size of your team, you may need accommodations for anywhere from 5 to 50 people. "House meetings" have always been a popular option for small community organizations. During the Civil Rights Movement, much of the strategic planning occurred in living rooms or around the dinner table. When houses were insufficient or unavailable, organizations would reach out to churches for meeting space. Today, many churches are still willing to provide rooms for community meetings, especially if some of your members are affiliated with the congregation.

Alternatively, there may be community centers, libraries, colleges, or museums in your town that will provide rooms for free or at a nominal cost. And while uncommon, occasionally local businesses are willing to share space as well, so consider all your options. The goal is to find a location that's consistently accessible to your group. You may have to sacrifice comfort for consistency to get started, but that's a safer bet than having meetings someplace you can't reliably afford or access.

That being said, depending on your resources you can usually rent conference rooms from hotels and social clubs (think Elks Lodge), and cheap office space may be found in low-income neighborhoods where typical businesses are afraid to operate. Call up and get a quote.

Oh, and be sure to check out your local Denny's.

HAVE FOOD (AND MUSIC)
Assuming you've found a space, food is the second most important part of any organizing meeting, and of course I will elaborate further.

First and foremost, food is a great motivator to get people to attend meetings. Never underestimate the effectiveness of a delicious food bribe. Food meetings can also be great time-savers by combining a meal with a discussion about the community.

In my organizing spaces, we have a dedicated food committee that works to ensure there is an abundance of goodies to munch on while we work. This is a high priority, as the act of breaking bread also helps us build bonds as a team and trust one another. In many cultures, communal eating is an intimate and sacred act among people in shared circumstances. Food is also a great way to get people to stay for discussions, as digestion takes some time and the act of eating can provide us with the endorphins necessary to power through.

But more importantly, people need food, and it's something that can and should be shared amongst comrades.

The first half hour of any meeting should be reserved for snacking and chatting, and allowing time for stragglers to arrive. Adding music is a nice touch to delineate this time from the rest of the meeting.

Since many of our members are low-income, we try to cover meal expenses with food stamps (SNAP), WIC, donated or rescued food, and other subsidies. We also regularly steal food for our meetings since pastries and snacks are relatively easy to smuggle out of supermarket storefronts. Food is a cost-effective, practical way to motivate and sustain your members and should be prioritized when planning any meeting.

Since the work of feeding people often falls on women due to patriarchy, it's important to ensure cis men are actively engaged in providing and contributing towards meals.

I personally don't excel at cooking, but I enjoy stealing food, utensils, tables, and other resources that go into food prep. I've also mastered the art of peeling and chopping potatoes and onions and washing dishes. And rumor has it I make a mean turkey sandwich. Just because someone isn't a chef doesn't mean they can't feed people.

CONSISTENCY IS KEY

Scheduling meetings will always be challenging under late-stage capitalism, where individuals have extremely limited time to dedicate to uncompensated labor. One way to address this is by holding consistent, recurring meetings for volunteer organizing. Having consistent meeting times allows us to plan our lives around meetings, rather than plan meetings around our chaotic lives. Start by asking core members which day of the week they are most likely to be available to meet. Prioritize the availability of the most marginalized members (Black women, single parents, disabled folks etc). Once a day and time are determined, schedule meetings to recur during that time slot on a recurring schedule. Try it out for a few weeks to see if it's viable before switching things up.

In my experience, weekly meetings are too frequent and can discourage attendance since people know another meeting is always seven days away. Conversely, monthly meetings are too far apart and can cause people to forget or become disinvested. The sweet spot seems to be hosting meetings every other week, on a consistent weekday. These are frequent enough that members will remember, and infrequent enough that they'll prioritize coming.

It doesn't matter if five people participate or 25, as long as the meetings are consistent. Attendance and productivity will shift based on the capacity and availability of members, as it should in any anti-capitalist framework. Send out meeting reminders to members in advance of every meeting, and always reiterate that attendance is voluntary. Pressuring or forcing people to come to meetings that they aren't eager to attend will only result in inefficiency and frustration.

HAVE AN AGENDA

A meeting outline or agenda is an effective way to help keep a meeting on track. It can be as simple as a Post-It note with three bullet points or as detailed as a multi-page document. A detailed agenda could include meeting discussion topics, community agreements, upcoming events, volunteer sign-up slots, political education readings, and puzzles or games in case participants need to zone out for a minute. Having printed agendas to hand out can make objectives more tangible and manageable to members. But agendas also help discussions stay on topic so that pressing items can be addressed and tasks can be assigned.

Structurally, agendas should use a large, clear font, and sensitive information should be omitted at all costs. If you're using agendas to plan activities that may be deemed illegal, it's probably a good idea to be as vague as possible and collect agendas at the end of meetings so they can't be used against you later on.

That being said, meeting agendas are simply a tool. They are guidelines, not gospel. Agendas can and should be deviated from and adjusted as needed, especially if unexpected issues arise before or during a given meeting.

A sample agenda can be found below. Feel free to take whatever is useful from this example. Build your own agenda to meet the needs of your organization and community.

> *"The most revolutionary thing one can do is always to proclaim loudly what is happening"* - Rosa Luxemburg

INTRO:
- Wellness Check + Intros (name, pronoun, prompt)
- Community Agreement Refresher for n00bs: Progressive Stack, Harm Buttons, Queer & Trans + Black and PoC affirming and prioritized space,
  Not a "secure space" and all collective discussions, ideas, suggestions, for the benefit of the community are public domain. Keep private, covert, or personal ideas to yourself.
  Be mindful of space and time used (limit long speeches, anecdotes, or diatribes)
- Local Food Rescue: Volunteer: 30 Main St. - Saturdays 11:30-2:30

THIS WEEK:
- **Report Backs**: Last week's Palestine Rally + recent Housing Justice Forum

3/30 Egg Hunt: SARATOGA VOLUNTEERS	CARLISLE VOLUNTEERS
9am:	9am:
12pm:	12pm:

- **May Event Planning:** Know Your Rights Training. Bystander Training. Safety Team + Medic Training. Tenant Rights? AutoRepair?
- **Upcoming Events**:
  - 3/30: Women's History Celebration at American Legion @ 4pm
  - 4/2: GloryShines Family Bowling Event @ 2pm
  - 4/15: SUNY BDS March in Albany @ 1pm // 4/20: Smoke Weed In Front of the Police Station
- Political Education: "The X-Men Comics, Transphobia, and Fascism." By Marc Burrows & Brett White

ACROSS →

1 Midnight visit to the kitchen
5 Quarterback's option
9 "Going once . . . Going twice . . . ___!"
13 Skin condition
14 "The Tortoise and the Hare," e.g.
15 "T," on a test
16 Collection of pictorial memories
18 Red, like a steak
19 Person who often has a lease
20 Flustered
22 Like most bubble tea
24 Columns with points of view
25 Kind of leaf on the Canadian flag
28 Colombian corn cake
32 Palindromic fashion magazine
33 Sensitive spots on the skin
34 Thumbs-downs
37 Living space with a single room
41 6-Down hit with the lyric 'Nothing else can save me"
42 Mystic letters
43 Vendor that supplies Wile E. Coyote with failure-prone products
44 Come into existence
45 Slightly off
46 Central point
50 Paul McCartney and Ian McKellen, e.g.
52 British spelling of a folded egg dish
56 Queens' domains
60 Nickname for a father
61 "Greetings for the second time!"
63 They might be fragile or inflated
64 Sticky tree substance
65 Italian volcano
66 Actor Rogen
67 Like hand-me-down clothes
68 "Rolling in the ___" (Adele song)

DOWN ↓

1 Spellbound
2 Feel sore
3 Involved with
4 Comprehensive
5 Word after "peri" or "gal"
6 Swedish band originally named Festfolk
7 Shell-less mollusk
8 Truck stop sight
9 Subway rider's handhold
10 Speak formally
11 Enticed
12 Homeowners' documents
14 Destiny
17 "You only live ___"
21 Base for smashed avocado, maybe
23 Evian alternative
25 Total dismay
26 Cher's vocal range
27 Bonos
29 Double Dutch needs
30 Hits the delete key
31 The "p" of mph
34 Guitar part with frets
35 "My treat!"
36 Dish such as th erid or sambar
38 Beyond mad
39 Your and my
40 Worked the knots out of
45 Field
46 Broods
47 Public relations concern
48 Home ___
49 Symbol that might mark a line break
51 Nutrient that tofu is high in
53 Drive-___ window
54 Some concert souvenirs
55 "What ___ is new?"
57 Not punctual
58 "Be ___" (candy heart message)
59 Velcro alternative
62 Pickle jar top

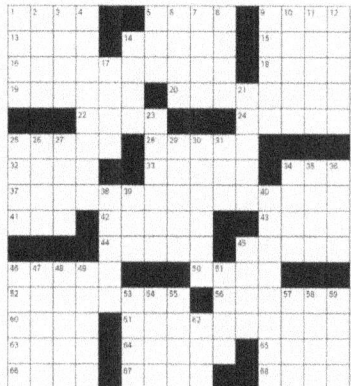

TAKE TURNS FACILITATING

Meeting facilitators are tasked with keeping a meeting on track and ensuring community guidelines and agreements are followed. Community agreements essentially refer to meeting etiquette, procedure, and decorum agreed upon at the start of every meeting. These guidelines are meant to structure the space in a way that prioritizes safety, equity, empathy, and productivity. Good facilitators guide a meeting but do not dictate the overall outcome or direction beyond reiterating agenda items and agreements.

Like any skill, learning facilitation takes time and practice. Alternating facilitators helps ensure others can employ this skill, while also preventing singular voices from dominating meeting spaces.

ACCOMMODATE CHILDREN

Space permitting, set a room aside for children to hang out, eat, and play during meetings. This pseudo-childcare will not only permit more parents to attend, it will acclimate children to the virtues of community and collaboration. Plus the sounds of children in the background make meetings feel less like a day at the office and more like a day at the park.

ACKNOWLEDGE HARM WHEN IT OCCURS

Whenever people gather, there's a likelihood of harm arising. In meeting spaces, this most often looks like somebody inadvertently saying something insensitive that's hurtful to others in the room. Harm is frequently addressed in shared spaces with the "Oops/Ouch Method"—which entails saying "Oops!" to pause the conversation and apologize if you've said something harmful, or saying "Ouch!" to pause the conversation if you feel you've been harmed.

I prefer the "Pause" method, in which any person in the room can pause a conversation in response to harm witnessed, experienced, or committed. For added flair and accessibility, cheap game show buzzers can be purchased and scattered around the room for people to press when harm occurs. These "harm buttons" can be a lighthearted way to acknowledge inadvertent harm and move on with the discussion. No, seriously.

But harm can also look like malicious and aggressive attacks, flagrant arguing, and insults meant to provoke violence. It's important to have protocols in place for addressing this more dangerous type of harm. Remove children and vulnerable people from the space. End the meeting if necessary. Employ de-escalation tactics and bystander intervention techniques when harm escalates to the point of provocation and abuse. And then take steps to protect future meetings from recurring instances.

INCORPORATE POLITICAL EDUCATION

Meetings aren't just a time to plan revolutionary work; they're a time to *employ* revolutionary work as well. To help sharpen a community's political views and praxis, political education can be incorporated into organizational meetings. Members can submit radical speeches, essays, book excerpts, and political cartoons that can be attached to upcoming agendas for group review and discussion. Ideally, these pieces would be short and accessible (no more than three pages) so they can be read aloud and discussed during a meeting. The idea is to encourage critical thinking, political analysis, practical application, and/or dissent within a given organizing space.

Incorporating political education into meetings is also a good way to engage and inspire members by applying a historical lens to current and ongoing issues. When we learn about the common struggle and our relationship to it, we're better prepared to protect ourselves and work as allies and accomplices in dismantling systems of oppression. Public meetings are an additional avenue for making political education more accessible and palatable to our comrades and cohorts.

NO COPS, NO OPS, NO ON-DUTY PRESS

Anytime a group of people conspire to disrupt capitalism, there will be risks involved. Meeting spaces are vulnerable to all manner of targeted attacks, infiltration, and harm from those who seek to see these spaces fail.

Just because an organization is open to new participants, doesn't mean it must subject its existing members to abuse.

Be discerning in who is permitted into these spaces, and create smaller spaces for core members who comprise the steering committee or team leadership; as well as sub-committees comprised of members from hypermarginalized demographics (Black Caucus, LGBTQ Caucus etc.). And as a general rule, basic vetting should take place to help prevent law enforcement and press from infiltrating organizational meetings.

To quote Malcolm X, "Put the white man out of our meetings, and then sit down and talk shop with each other. That's what we've got to do."

VIII

LIE, CHEAT, STEAL
THE IMPORTANCE OF BREAKING RULES

I dropped out of high school when I was 17. My mother's health had been rapidly deteriorating for some time, and my family was struggling in every way imaginable. Prior to dropping out, I would frequently skip class to pick up extra shifts at a local supermarket to help with the bills.

I hated high school but aspired to attend college where I could take evening classes and free up more of my days to work. It was my high school guidance counselor who suggested I take the GED exam and try to enroll in college rather than simply dropping out. She informed me that to take the GED exam before my graduation date I would first have to prove my competence by passing a practice test. She then graciously called the Adult Learning Center on my behalf and scheduled my practice exam for the same day. My counselor was confident I'd pass, and frankly, so was I.

I wasn't a stellar high school student for a myriad of reasons, but I was relatively astute and liked taking tests. When I was diagnosed with autism in middle school, I remember one of the questions asked was if I enjoyed exams, which I enthusiastically confirmed.

For me, completing an exam is like finishing a jigsaw puzzle. I love the simplicity of the process and the feeling of accomplishment that goes with it. I enjoy the fact I can complete a test at my own pace and not the pace of the instructor or other students in the class. I love finishing first and slamming my pencil down like an asshole. So when I received a perfect score on the practice GED exam later that afternoon, I remember feeling satisfied and eager to tell my guidance counselor.

There was only one problem: My score was too high.

My counselor informed me that some of the financial aid I'd need to pay for college—like the stipends from the Educational Opportunity Program (EOP)—were only available to students who were low-income AND ineligible for admission under traditional academic standards—i.e., "students who fall slightly below the criteria for general admission."

It wasn't enough to live in poverty; I also had to be a 'D' student. If I got a perfect score on my official GED exam, I'd be disqualified from receiving those financial aid packages and other resources I'd need to attend university. I'd have to score between 63% and 69% to be eligible for the maximum amount of aid.

To rectify this, I calculated exactly how many questions I'd need to answer *incorrectly* in order to game the system. All I had to do was leave those questions blank—and answer all the other questions right—to ensure a score low enough to qualify for the additional aid, but high enough to pass the exam. Piece of cake.

When I took the official exam two weeks later, I managed to score exactly 67%, which was somehow more gratifying than receiving a perfect score.

I never questioned the ethics of manipulating my test results in exchange for tuition money because I was a 17-year-old kid desperately trying to claw my way out of poverty. And to an extent, it worked. I dropped out of high school and went on to graduate from college with high honors, and had I not bent the rules to do so, my life would have turned out much differently.

As I've gotten older and dedicated much of my time to advocacy and resistance, I've learned that breaking rules is often the only way to get ahead. The hard part was coming to that realization and embracing it, despite the risks.

If you haven't guessed by now, the text you're currently reading was largely inspired by *Steal This Book* by Abbie Hoffman. *Steal This Book* is a must-read for anyone looking to radically transform society through unconventional means. Much of Hoffman's work focuses on undermining capitalism through crime and opportunism, and despite being more than 50 years old, many of the concepts discussed are still relevant today.

In fact, Hoffman's work has arguably become more relevant over time, as wealth inequality in the United States has worsened exponentially. According to the U.S. Census Bureau, nearly 40 million Americans were living in poverty as of 2023, compared to 25 million in the early 1970s when *Steal This Book* was first published. Additionally, according to the U.S. Bureau of Labor Statistics, the federal minimum wage in 2025 (adjusted for inflation) is more than 40%(!) *lower* than the minimum wage in 1971.

The more people struggle under capitalism, the more likely communities are to resort to all manner of crime and deception to survive. This is widely accepted and understood across the political spectrum. The US Department of Justice openly acknowledges that "The percent of families below the poverty level positively correlates with both violent crime and property crime rates." And in many states, the criminalization of poverty has led to an increase in new crimes that previously wouldn't have been deemed illegal—like camping outdoors, sleeping in your car, or "loafing."

Crime, however, isn't just a byproduct of poverty, it's also a viable means of combating the circumstances that *create* poverty (i.e. capitalism). Because of this, criminalization will often target acts of survival as well as acts of resistance.

In Houston, for example, an ordinance was passed making it illegal to feed five or more people without a permit. This applies to feeding the homeless but also includes giving food to protestors occupying a public space, which could result in a $500 per day fine. Laws like this are becoming commonplace all over the country, despite being at odds with the First Amendment right to assembly.

As Dr. King noted, "One has a moral responsibility to disobey unjust laws." Those in power know that civil disobedience on any large scale poses a real threat to the status quo. If breaking laws is normalized or encouraged to any significant extent (like we saw in the civil unrest of 2020), society would be at risk of collapse. And since capitalism inherently requires suffering and exploitation, which inevitably lead to crime, police and governments are tasked with keeping dissent at a manageable level through state violence.

If and when those levels become unmanageable, only then do social change and appeasement occur. **Therefore, crimes or acts of rebellion that challenge institutional power are not only good for society, they are necessary for any successful revolution.**

Crime is of the essence.

As community organizers, we must be willing to think outside the box to acquire and redistribute the resources necessary to sustain not only resistance, but our survival. And before anyone accuses me of promoting criminal activity, I'd like to clarify that that's exactly what I'm doing. Let's get into it.

LIE TO LANDLORDS

Housing has been increasingly difficult to secure thanks to the ongoing landlord crisis. Lying to landlords is one way to subvert capitalism in order to attain housing. This most often looks like modifying pay stubs to make it appear as if your income is "three times the rent." Landlords prefer renting to single, pet-free, child-free, non-smokers with disposable income. The more you can convince them this is you, even if it's not, the easier it will be to get the keys to an apartment.

In Liberal-leaning states, signing the lease is often the biggest housing challenge, as there are protections in place to prevent (or at least delay) swift evictions. Get your foot in the door first and sort out the details later.

Also, landlords are lazy. Unless there's an urgent or costly repair for them to make, consider doing basic maintenance on your own to prevent them from routinely accessing your apartment. This may seem counterproductive, but the less work they have to do, the safer you will be, and the less inclined they will be to evict or interact with you. Pestering landlords generally results in them finding reasons to get rid of tenants, rather than them making the repairs. They don't need to know every little thing happening in your apartment. So replace your own shower heads and lightbulbs if you can. Tighten screws when warranted. Coordinate with your neighbors to perform simple maintenance and repairs. And do what you can to keep landlords far away from your rental unit.

LIE TO EMPLOYERS

If you're seeking employment, lying to prospective employers is a time-tested means of landing a job. Gaps in your resume? Fill them in by extending the start and end dates of past positions. Employers are unlikely to verify prior employment, and even less likely to verify the exact dates. If, during an interview, you're asked, "What would your current or former employer say about you?" lie like a rug. You want to come off like you're *eager* for them to call and check your references and credentials.

Projecting confidence that your former employers loved you can discourage future employers from doing too much digging. The more confidence you exude, the less likely they are to call your bluff. The worst thing you can do is answer honestly and say you got fired from a job because you hated every waking minute of it or "weren't a good fit."

Make up respectable reasons for leaving: "I wanted to pursue school," "I wanted more opportunities for advancement." "I needed to take time off to care for my grandmother, who passed away last month." It doesn't matter what you say, as long as it makes you sound like a viable candidate. Employers are not people, so it's OK to lie to them to get your foot in the door.

LIE TO POLICE

Generally speaking, you should never speak to the police. If you're questioned, stick with the basics: "Am I being detained? Am I free to go? Do you have a warrant? I'd like an attorney." But sometimes it's fun and prudent to lie to the police if it can help other people get out of trouble.

Once, I watched an older woman get apprehended by law enforcement while stealing diapers and baby food from a local grocer. I interjected myself into the arrest and said I knew the woman from church and offered to pay for the stolen groceries or accompany her to the police station if they insisted on pressing charges. The police ended up letting her off with a warning because they didn't want the hassle of a third party getting involved. The woman was beyond grateful that somebody was willing to lie to help her avoid arrest.

If you see a teenager fleeing the police, point in the opposite direction and yell "He went that way!" If a vehicle is receiving a parking ticket, run up and say "I'm here, officer!" and pretend to look for your keys. If you're open to the idea of perjury, offer to take the witness stand to help your friend win a criminal trial. The possibilities are endless. Bystander interventions take many forms, and lying to police is one way to undermine authority. It's always OK to lie to oppressors.

HIJACK LOCAL MEETINGS
When local government entities (City Council, School Board, County Legislature, etc) host public meetings there's often what's known as the "public comment portion." Ignore those. Community members don't have to sit quietly waiting for our turn to be heard—especially when discussing matters of life and death. Rules of decorum are just another way to silence residents in public spaces.

If you organize well and have enough support with you, any meeting can be hijacked by a vocal community. Disrupt meetings if warranted and set your own agenda. Ignore the time limits. The government is supposed to work for us. Not the other way around. (Plus it's fun.)

SHOPLIFT
Shoplifting is an important skill to develop whether you're a community organizer or just someone trying to save money. It's also a personal hobby of mine. Many of the community events I've coordinated over the years have been stocked almost entirely with "liberated" goods.

Liberating resources is an essential component of revolutionary work, but also an important tool for survival. With that in mind, everything I've written up until this point was mainly so I'd have an excuse to sneak shoplifting tips into a book. Enjoy!

Twenty Two Tips for Shoplifting:

1.   Be an opportunist. Steal things that are low-risk by taking advantage of opportunities that present themselves. When you walk into a store, make a mental note of items near the door that are easy to swipe on your way out. The idea is to steal things that are easy and accessible, but will add up over time. You won't have much success if you only go around stealing high-ticket items under lock and key. It's smarter to steal cheap things consistently so you can afford to pay for higher ticket items as needed.

2.   Never pay for anything smaller than your hand. As a rule of thumb, you shouldn't pay for anything that can be concealed in your hand. Travel-sized items are your friend: batteries, soap, toothpaste, makeup, small tools, candy, cheese, etc. True story: I haven't paid for deodorant since the Obama administration. Things that easily fit in your hand will easily disappear into your purse or pockets. They don't call it a Five Finger Discount for nothing. Grab and go!

3.   Dress the part. Try to dress in a way that will avoid suspicion. That usually means dressing like a "respectable" or upscale citizen. Cut the lining out of coats so you can fill the inseam with goods. Wear loose-fitting "mens" clothing when possible, because they have large pockets. Stealing things by hiding them on your person remains the safest way to shoplift, because staff don't like running the risk of searching you and being wrong.

4.   Act like you're shopping. The goal is to look like a shopper. Grab a shopping cart when you walk in and put a few items in it. People who walk around with a cart are less likely to be followed or watched by security because they look like typical shoppers. You can abandon this cart later once you've acquired what you actually came to steal. Everyone buys bananas, so they make a good decoy in a supermarket. Just make sure there's something in your cart. Check your shopping list periodically as you walk around the store to really ramp up the performance. If you walk in empty-handed while wearing a trench coat and sunglasses, you're going to arouse suspicion.

5.   Assume you're being watched. Don't pocket items in the aisles where they're found. Put things in your pockets or purse as you're walking around the store to make it harder to track your movements. The hygiene/electronics aisles always have more cameras than the underwear/baking aisles, so make sure you're pocketing things in low-profile areas that are less likely to have surveillance.

6.   Have an exit plan. Choose large stores with multiple exits when possible. Try to limit shoplifting from small local stores or bodegas, since they're generally harder to steal from (and if you get caught, you'll lose access to a neighborhood resource). Go in one entrance and walk out the opposite door when you leave, or choose the exit that has the least observant security guard/greeter. Multiple exits mean you'll have options for your escape.

7. **Always have a receipt on you.** Keep a clean receipt in your pocket that you can take out as you exit a store. This is particularly useful for stealing large items or even full shopping carts. Simply holding a receipt—any receipt—puts people at ease and dispels suspicion. Many times, an employee has gone to approach me to check my bag or cart and stopped when they saw me holding a white slip of paper. For added effect, bring a department store item to the most clueless-looking cashier while carrying a faux receipt in your hand, and tell the cashier you'd like to return the item. The flustered cashier will likely direct you to the Customer Service Desk, at which point you say "Thank you!" and walk right out the door.

8. **Keep walking/Don't look back.** Don't stop for greeters. Don't stop to have someone check your receipt. Don't stop if someone calls after you. Once you exit the store, make a bee-line to depart. If you hesitate or give store security more time to question you or call the police, it will only work against you. Unless you're physically stopped and apprehended, consider yourself free to go and keep walking.

9. **Avoid security tags.** Cheaper items are less likely to have security tags that set off alarms when you exit the store. If you can remove the tag, that's great, but sometimes they're inside the package and you won't be able to see them. Removing tags and packaging from an item while it's in your pocket is a good way to prevent an item from triggering an alarm. But as mentioned above, even if you hear an alarm as you exit, KEEP WALKING.

10. Know the store's layout. Knowing the general layout of a store can help you move quickly and confidently. You don't want to waste precious moments roaming around looking for items and asking for help. You want to walk in and get out ASAP. Get familiar with stores in your area and do preliminary reconnaissance missions to find items in advance of stealing them. While there, take note of staffing levels and what employees are up to. Stores that are short-staffed are gold mines for shoplifters, and as a bonus, they generally don't pay their employees a living wage, so they deserve to get ripped off. Win/win!

11. Pretend you're absent-minded. If you do get questioned, pretend you were simply distracted and made a mistake. This won't always get you out of trouble, but it works more often than you'd think.

12. Don't steal from self-checkout. I know this one hurts. For the past several years, surveillance technology has been collecting data and tracking our movements at self-checkout. It's gotten so sophisticated that it's really not worth stealing from this area of the store. It's best to steal while you're walking around the store amongst the merchandise, or from the entryway as you leave. Even if you get away with stealing from self-checkout, it's likely the store filmed your theft and archived it for later. Larger retailers are compiling evidence over time so they can charge thieves with felonies for collective and recurring heists. Stealing consistently from self-checkout is a good way to end up behind bars.

13. Be quick. Have an idea of what you're coming to steal before you walk into the store. If it's only one or two items, it's totally reasonable to be out of the store in 90 seconds. Time yourself.

14. Diversify your targets. Stealing from the same one or two stores over and over again is a surefire way to get caught. If you have access to reliable transportation, travel between stores to help stay off the radar of store security. Don't always go at the same time of day or day of the week. The more you spread out your heists, the harder you will be to catch.

15. Go to rich neighborhoods. Stores in the suburbs generally have less security. That being said, certain high-profile retail stores can have very sophisticated security systems. Be observant. Chit-chat with employees to get a sense of how good security is at a certain location. Stores with good security generally get a reputation for being difficult to steal from. Avoid them when possible.

16. Rush hour is prime time. The busier the store, generally the easier it will be to steal. When a store is bustling, the employees and management are usually too busy to keep a watchful eye. Take advantage of the rush hour cover.

17. Use other distractions. In addition to rush hour, any disturbance can serve as a good diversion to help you make a clean getaway. You can take advantage of a random occurrence—an argument in the store, a power failure, a traffic accident in the parking lot—or you can create your own by working in teams. Have one person walk around acting suspicious, being loud, knocking over displays, and/or talking to management/security, while another less conspicuous person walks out the door with the goods. Whenever the attention isn't on you is the safest time to grab and go.

18. Get rid of any evidence. Once you make it out safely, drop your items off somewhere quickly. If you're walking or driving around town with stolen merchandise on you, it will only give the police more ammunition to charge you. It's possible (but unlikely) that cops may track you down based on your license plate or photo and show up at your door. So make sure any packaging is out of sight and any items are put away. Don't get caught with a pile of unopened merchandise on your porch.

19. Know when to abort the mission. If you have a bad feeling or get a sense that you're being watched, abort the mission. Ditch any merchandise and exit the store. Trust your instincts.

20. Kids shouldn't shoplift. Sorry, kids. Shoplifting as a juvenile is pointless. Everyone expects young people to steal and unsupervised children are easy targets for law enforcement and store security. The best advice I have for young rebels is to wait until they're grown, and leave the thievery to us older folks in the meantime.

21. Lean into your privilege. Conversely, those with excess privilege should shoplift every chance they get. If you can navigate the world without raising suspicion, use that to your advantage. That means white people, the elderly, conventionally attractive people, employed people, formally educated people, and those with class and social standing. The more you steal, the more you'll have to contribute to those with less freedom and privilege in society. Shoplift today and pay it forward tomorrow.

22. PRACTICE! The hardest part of shoplifting is finding the courage to move with confidence. Practice by walking into a dollar store and swiping some ChapStick or gum. Small, low-risk grabs prepare us for the big leagues, but more importantly, add up over time. If you steal regularly it will become a habit, and that will help you become more confident.

Remember, these are merely tips for successful shoplifting, not rules. The only rule for shoplifting is "Don't get caught." Happy hunting!

IX

ABOUT THE ROACHES
THE NEVERENDING DEBATE ON TAKING RISKS

On June 7, 2022, hundreds of massive cockroaches were released into an Albany, New York, courthouse, forcing an emergency evacuation and suspension of all scheduled proceedings for the day.

A dubia cockroach (*blaptica dubia*) is a large tropical insect native to select regions of South America. Adult dubia roaches can grow to nearly two inches long—roughly the size of a human thumb. The males have partially functional wings they can use to slow their descent from trees and other tall objects, should they lose their footing.

They're not particularly pleasant looking, but generally speaking, dubia roaches are harmless, odorless, flightless, fruit-loving insects that are non-invasive to most climates. Because they're so easy to breed in captivity, they've become a popular feeder insect among reptile enthusiasts... such as myself.

In Albany, a colony of full-grown dubia roaches was allegedly smuggled into the main courtroom by a disgruntled protestor in response to video footage of New York State Troopers violently assaulting a disabled Black woman a few weeks prior. The roach release coincided with early morning arraignment proceedings related to that incident. Upon their release, chaos ensued.

When the swarm was first noticed by attendees, screams could reportedly be heard echoing throughout the courthouse as witnesses clamored for the nearest exits to escape the infestation.

Police initially attempted to stop the spread by corralling the roaches with brooms and other objects. When that failed, they tried stomping on the plump insects—one by one—in a bid to neutralize the intrusion. According to witnesses, this strategy only succeeded in creating a sticky mess on the floor, prompting one officer to yell, "Stop, they're too big!"

Undeterred, the frenzied pests continued to swarm throughout the building, starting from the main courtroom and proceeding throughout the judge's chambers and adjoining offices. Maintenance workers eventually arrived with an industrial ShopVac and attempted to suck up the individual roaches that were still visible, but by then it was too late. They were everywhere; the courthouse had to be shut down for the day.

Word of the incident spread nearly as quickly as the critters themselves, eventually reaching national and international news outlets.

"What transpired today is not advocacy or activism, it is criminal behavior with the intent to disrupt a proceeding and cause damage," read a statement from the Office of Court Administration as reported by *The Huffington Post*.

To date, the assailant has not been caught.

The fallout from this incident was varied. At a governmental level, the Albany Police Department and Albany Criminal Court were embarrassed and mocked by neighboring departments for succumbing to the disruption. Due to the security breach, new policies were put in place to more thoroughly screen members of the public upon entering the courthouse.

The Governor's Office reportedly got involved to demand answers as to how an "attack" like this could occur in the State Capitol without so much as a conviction. One seasoned organizer was arrested for allegedly coordinating a diversion in the court, but those charges were ultimately dismissed. The global news coverage effectively raised the profile of the initial incident and put additional scrutiny on the department's failings.

Among local organizers, many felt the stunt was justified, especially since it was in response to a violent police assault on a vulnerable community member. But there was also a discussion on whether the deployment of the roaches was a step "too far," given that the action wasn't pre-approved by other protestors in attendance.

Furthermore, some deemed the tactic reckless, crude, unnecessarily gross, and even harmful to animals. But the biggest criticism was regarding if it was worth the risks involved with shutting down a major courthouse just to dramatize a point about the pervasiveness of State violence.

"What if a community member was injured during the rush for the exits?" "What if somebody was arrested and aggressively charged?" "What if the police had responded violently?" These are all valid questions to ask when engaging in civil disobedience and direct action. There are inherent risks involved in agitation, and those risks should always be considered and weighed.

My personal observation is that, most often, caution wins out over risk-taking—and for good reason. The risks associated with civil disobedience have grown increasingly harsh in recent years, as the state seeks to quell and discourage resistance before it occurs.

In the early days of the Black Lives Matter Movement, mass arrests were relatively infrequent, but when they did occur, the charges were often violations or petty misdemeanors. During the Ferguson uprisings following the 2014 murder of Mike Brown, for example, most of the 160 or so individuals arrested were solely charged with "Failure to Disperse"—a low-level misdemeanor.

More than a decade later, it's not uncommon for demonstrators to be charged with serious felonies during large protests. Recently, at least 42 people demonstrating against the new "Cop City" training facility in Atlanta were charged with "Domestic Terrorism," which carries a penalty of up to 35 years in prison.

But high risks associated with radical organizing are nothing new, and American prisons are still holding freedom fighters from the 1970s and '80s who paid the ultimate price for their commitment to the Revolution.

Mutulu Shakur was one such freedom fighter imprisoned for his alleged role in helping Assata Shakur escape from Clinton Correctional Facility in 1979. Mutulu was captured and convicted in 1988. He served 37 years before finally being released in 2023, only to die seven months later from blood cancer. He spent most of his life in prison as a result of the risks he was willing to take as a young man. Assata Shakur remains free to this day.

Nine years prior to Mutulu helping Assata Shakur escape, another risky action took place 300 miles South of Clinton Correctional Facility, this one at Lincoln Hospital in the Bronx. The action involved nearly 200 Black and Puerto Rican radicals—led by the Young Lords—taking over the hospital in a bid to improve horrendous care conditions for patients. Their 12-hour occupation successfully drew attention to the disparate state of healthcare in the South Bronx, which helped accelerate the building of a new Lincoln Hospital a few years later. Two lead organizers were arrested for their involvement in the occupation, but their charges were ultimately dropped—a significantly different outcome when compared to that of Mutulu Shakur.

The bold actions of Mutulu Shakur and the Young Lords are equal parts aspirational and inspirational, despite the numerous risks and sacrifices involved. When considering the scope of these historical acts of resistance, I can't help but question persistent claims that the risks associated with contemporary resistance are "too high." I believe risk assessment varies wildly from person to person, and determinations must be made on an individual basis.

"We have to be clear around the risks we face when we confront the state," writes veteran organizer and journalist, Justin A. Davis, "and I think that's one of the lessons of [...] political prisoners. When you take a step back and assess what they were up to and what brought on state repression, it's not very different than the organizing that we're doing today."

Increasingly, there are factions of society that claim to be in favor of justice and social progress, but reject any and all radical means to bring about lasting change. They're against "unlawful" protests, occupations and encampments, riots, vandalism, public agitation, and anything that may result in arrest or injury. Generally, these entities have varied levels of comfort and/or privilege that they are unwilling to compromise for the greater good. They're not conservatives in the typical sense, but they still have something to conserve. They'll co-opt and exploit Leftist verbiage, but the similarities end there. These entities not only abstain from radical organizing, they actively *discourage* others who seek to bring about change in ways that may carry greater risks. And in a grand twist of irony, they put marginalized people at greater risk by doing so.

Out of resentment, insecurity, fear, or a combination of the three, these groups will take the path of least resistance while simultaneously declaring their commitment to the Struggle. Their inaction alone is not necessarily detrimental to liberation work, but discouraging acts of resistance solely because an individual or entity is unable to bear the consequences is ahistorical, impractical, and counter-revolutionary. It is in this way that liberalism enables fascism.

Be wary of self-proclaimed Leftists who only seek to deter radical organizing efforts due to the presumed risks, because the most marginalized members of society face risks regardless of their level of involvement in movement work. The state makes it a point to brandish and amplify the consequences of dissent at every opportunity to frighten us into compliance. Despite this, oppressed people of all ages and races regularly face these consequences head-on, in the pursuit of justice.

In Birmingham, for example, during the Riots of 1963, children as young as nine would skip school to confront police dogs and fire hoses during the mass uprisings. Teenagers were even known to carry toothbrushes when they marched, signifying to police that they were ready and willing to spend the night in jail if need be. The actions of these children were nothing short of revolutionary. There were some, however, who dismissed these brave young people as cavalier thrill seekers intent on taking unnecessary risks. These nay-sayers would have been mistaken then, just as they are mistaken now.

Similarly, the bus boycotts of the 1950s were risky and illegal, resulting in nearly 100 arrests, but they also accomplished the desegregation of public buses and forced the Supreme Court to rule against segregation nationally. The Stonewall Uprising of 1969, which also resulted in dozens of arrests and injuries, sparked a cultural shift that led to the formation of several organizations for LGBTQ rights that paved the way for marriage equality, and increased the visibility and representation of queer people in mainstream culture. By 2016, Manhattan's Stonewall Inn was declared a national monument and shortly thereafter, a formal apology was issued by New York's police commissioner.

As the saying goes, "Direct action gets the goods."

Political education alone does not bring about change. Raising awareness does not guarantee justice. And being morally right does nothing to ensure progress. "Nobody in the world, nobody in history, has ever gotten their freedom by appealing to the moral sense of the people who were oppressing them," writes Assata Shakur. Indeed, Shakur's freedom was not attained through rhetoric, but through action.

Opting out of taking risks is a privilege afforded to few. The goal is to live long and freely, not to forfeit ourselves for a hypothetical future, but for many, these paths are intertwined. As abolitionist Frederick Douglass noted, "If there is no struggle, there is no progress." To put it plainly, some things are worth the risks. Rhetorical demands make clear our expectations, but without bold action, there is zero incentive for the state to concede to our collective will.

One last anecdote: In 2018, I briefly worked as an analyst for the New York State Department of Transportation. My job was to secure funding for highway repairs and maintenance. Routinely, we'd be made aware of an intersection or roadway that posed an imminent danger to the public due to structural decay or environmental factors. Residents would often plead for our agency to fix these treacherous roads before somebody got killed. And routinely those pleas would be ignored due to lack of funding to address the deficiency.

As it turned out, the fastest way to secure resources from the State was for a fatality to occur at a given location. It was common to sit in meetings and hear, "Good news, somebody finally died at this intersection, so we can advance construction." Predictably, I was fired within a year.

The state's only priority is self-preservation, so once there is an outcome that has the potential to be a liability (like a death on a major roadway or a hospital overrun by radicals), only then will those in power respond. Spilled blood literally dictates budgets and fuels revolutions. This notion was plainly stated by Malcolm X in 1963, when he declared, "You haven't got a revolution that doesn't involve bloodshed." My time working as a government employee helped solidify my understanding that the state must be *forced* into serving The People™—even in matters of life and death.

As such, we should all strive to be liabilities to oppression in spite of the risks, because the biggest risk of all...

...is doing nothing.

X

SHOWTIME!
COORDINATING COMMUNITY EVENTS

On March 31st, 2021, New York became the 15th state to legalize recreational cannabis use.

To celebrate, my friends and I threw a weed festival directly in front of the Binghamton Police Station on 4/20. Roughly 700 people attended.

The 1st Annual Smoke Weed in Front of the Binghamton Police Station

The "Smoke Weed in Front of the Binghamton Police Station" event was first and foremost a political rally meant to raise awareness about the decriminalization of pot, as well as an opportunity to put the new law into practice. But it was also an excuse to get responsibly baked in front of a bunch of cops who couldn't do anything about it (more on that later).

The event included musical performances, free food, political education, NARCAN training for overdose prevention, and lots and lots of weed. The police and mayor's office hated it, the community loved it, and overall, we had a great time.

Coordinating this event took the combined efforts of a dozen or so talented organizers committed to our ambitious vision of getting high in public. Pulling it off in only 20 days required the deployment of existing infrastructure and resources we'd built up over the years, complete with a dedicated safety team, street medics, legal observers, political educators, and vendors. It was a lot of work, but we had the necessary tools at our disposal and the will of The People™ to get it done. Without those things, this event would have been another compelling idea among a slew of compelling ideas to never materialize.

Truth be told, coming up with ideas is often the easiest part of organizing an event. Putting those ideas into action is much more challenging, especially when your target audience is everyone struggling under capitalism.

Technically, we could have pulled this particular event off with a few joints and a lighter, but the significance to the community would have been greatly diminished. And if we're going to rally people to come together, we want to make sure mass gatherings are thoughtful, engaging, and most of all, empowering. This requires actively and intentionally challenging institutional power and the status quo. It also requires being careful not to collaborate with fascist organizations or government entities who frequently gatekeep communal resources.

We held our weed festival for three years straight without incident. Each year it grew more and more radical in its messaging and bravado.

In the fourth year, we anticipated a crowd of over a thousand, with visitors coming in from all over the country; but instead, an army of sheriff's deputies descended upon the masses and violently arrested 14 participants, including elders and the disabled. I was among those arrested and spent much of the day in jail. Those in power recognized what we were doing, and sought to put an end to it once and for all.

By arresting so many people, local officials were attempting to send a message to the community that dissent and mockery of the state would not be tolerated. But it was too late. People had come to love our annual act of resistance and joy, and had learned to appreciate the spirit of camaraderie and defiance on display. The arrests only brought further shame and mockery to the very institutions we sought to undermine. And they brought the community closer together. Mission accomplished.

Organizers aren't event planners for the sake of simply planning events. The goal is to create spaces for communities to learn, grow, and build collectively. The goal is nothing short of total liberation. The powers that be would prefer we never congregated nor exchanged resources and ideas. They'd prefer we only went to work and school, spent money in between, and died before collecting Social Security. Large communal gatherings are therefore inherently radical. They are also simultaneously a way to gauge our outreach capabilities and deficiencies, and assess our capacity for mobilization. And gathering consistently helps us prepare for future events that will inevitably transpire.

When the George Floyd uprisings occurred in 2020, for example, nothing was going to stop folks from pouring into the streets. But communities that already had experience coming together for a common cause were at an advantage, politically and organizationally. In other words, we're safer when we practice this stuff. **A community of strangers is a community at risk.**

As such, mass mobilization is a serious undertaking. Organizers have to factor in logistics, safety, accessibility, resources, and practicality. We also have to assess community interest and sentiment surrounding the theme(s) of the event to determine if it's warranted or appropriate for the given circumstances. A weed festival on 4/20 celebrating legalization is kind of a no-brainer. But often, the decision to throw an event simply comes down to how badly community members and organizers want it to happen.

If you don't have the resources (including volunteers) necessary to pull off an event, it's time to either start gathering those resources or start scaling back the scope of the initiative. Often our ideas are larger than our budgets and limitations, but that's OK. The goal is to do what we can with what we have at our disposal. Our resources shouldn't dictate our commitment. Don't bite off more than you can chew, but don't sell yourself short, either. Oh, and have faith. If you build it, something something…

Assuming you already have the resources and you've determined the needs of your community (Chapter 6), and also created meeting spaces to hash out your priorities and undertakings (Chapter 7), it's probably time to start coordinating events.

Frequently, community events fall under three distinct categories: **Community Preparedness**, **Rapid Response**, and **Community Engagement**. I'll outline them below. Please keep in mind this list is not exhaustive, and there's often significant overlap among events. But generally speaking, if you're a grassroots organizer you'll most often be organizing one or more of the following. So let's jump right in.

COMMUNITY PREPAREDNESS

Communities reliant on the state for survival cannot successfully undermine state oppression. As such, Community Preparedness initiatives are meant to improve or advance community sustainability and foster the skills needed to survive (and eventually overthrow) capitalism. These can be recurring events, like weekly workshops or food distribution initiatives, or individual political trainings and skillshares. Community Preparedness events aren't inherently centered around recreation or socialization, although those components are often incorporated. These initiatives should educate and inform a community, and ultimately help it become more self-sufficient.

Community Preparedness initiatives are also meant to mitigate communal *harm*, rather than *crime*. This distinction is important.

Communal harm is a detriment to the wellbeing of people in a given community. Hunger, houselessness, domestic violence, and drug overdoses are examples of communal harm. Crime, on the other hand, is a legal classification of actions that often pose a threat to property, as opposed to people. Shoplifting, vandalism, vagrancy, and public urination are examples of crimes that don't necessarily pose a legitimate threat to the well-being of others. While some harm may constitute crime, not all crime constitutes harm. For this reason, "neighborhood watch" initiatives that promote surveillance and reliance on law enforcement to protect property do *not* fall under the realm of Community Preparedness.

The Black Panthers were masters of Community Preparedness, and many of their initiatives sought to address communal harm. As noted by anarchist author Kristian Williams, "As much as they were concerned about the police, the Panthers also [...] sought to address the fears of the community they served. With this in mind, they organized Seniors Against a Fearful Environment (SAFE), an escort and busing service in which young Black people accompanied the elderly on their business around the city." These endeavors intended to make neighborhoods safer, as well as promote self-reliance and communal autonomy through preparedness.

Common styles of Community Preparedness initiatives fall under the realm of **Trainings & Workshops** and **Mutual Aid** initiatives.

- **Training & Workshop** topics may include bystander intervention, safety team, street medic & basic first aid, stop the bleed training, wilderness survival, auto repair, self defense, firearms training, civil disobedience, base building, anti-racism, and cyber security. Teach-ins, lectures, and skillshares of all kinds are also included in this category.

- **Mutual Aid** initiatives include escort teams, free childcare, community gardens, cooperative food banks, public food pantries, community shelves, clothing swaps, free stores, donation drives and give-a-ways, ride shares, letter writing/pen pal initiatives, book exchange programs, street libraries, the Black Panthers' Free Breakfast Program and the Young Lords' "Garbage Offensive."

As a general guideline, Community Preparedness initiatives should incorporate some facets of political education to foster a shared understanding of what, exactly, communities are preparing for—and why. Political education can be formal or informal and doesn't always look like trainings or workshops.

During the 1920s and '30s, political education often took the form of orators conducting lectures and speeches on street corners. Hubert Harrison was one such street orator who, during the Harlem Renaissance, regularly caused traffic jams in Manhattan due to the size of the crowds he could draw by simply lecturing about Black politics and philosophy. Similarly, in Chicago, anarchist and educator Lucy Parsons would incite large crowds with her biting political commentary and rousing rhetoric. Parsons' speeches were so compelling they prompted Chicago police to label her "more dangerous than a thousand rioters."

Whether a workshop, a street-safety initiative, or an impassioned speech, educating the masses remains an art form that requires practice and consistency if we hope to better prepare our communities.

RAPID RESPONSE

Rapid Response initiatives are meant to address an immediate need, threat, or current event impacting a vulnerable community or marginalized group. The most common example would be a political protest. These events are often highly visible, serving as tentpoles of radical community agendas while constituting a relatively small portion of overall organizational work.

Rapid Response initiatives are typically fueled by a sense of urgency present in a community during or immediately following an injustice or an ongoing human rights violation. They can be theatrical, disruptive, cathartic and/or subdued, depending on the catalyst.

Types of Rapid Response endeavors include: **Protests**, **Direct Actions**, **Vigils**, and **Eviction Defense**.

- **Protest & Direct Actions** include mass gatherings and specific acts meant to draw attention to a given injustice, and/or put pressure on the entities responsible. Protests & Direct Actions often incorporate acts of civil disobedience—from occupying public spaces to shutting down roadways and toppling oppressive monuments. These events generally receive much more attention than the less dramatic socio-political initiatives related to Community Preparedness.

- **Vigils** are healing spaces created in response to a tragedy or harmful event impacting a given community. They are generally peaceful gatherings for reflection and processing of shared trauma.

- **Eviction Defense** initiatives are a specific type of direct action meant to delay or prevent an impending eviction. These actions are most often coordinated by a local tenants union, housing justice org, or concerned neighbors attempting to advocate for a vulnerable tenant.

Rapid Response initiatives are quite literally a reaction to injustice, so they are sometimes dismissed as "reactionary" in the pejorative sense. But reacting to abuse is natural and often warranted among survivors and those most impacted. Furthermore, because of their high visibility, Rapid Response initiatives are a proven way to galvanize and empower communities, and also boost recruitment— all while simultaneously disrupting the status quo.

Still, Rapid Response initiatives must be employed thoughtfully and sparingly, as they run the risk of depleting the entirety of resources and energy available for grassroots organizing. Much like charity work, Rapid Response undertakings are primarily triage efforts necessary to keep a movement alive during tumultuous times. They're vital, but cannot constitute the majority of our efforts, as that would be unsustainable.

As a security measure, be careful not to credit individuals when organizing and promoting these types of actions, since they are often deemed unlawful. The last thing you want are police knocking on your door two days after a rowdy protest asking why your name was on the flyer.

COMMUNITY ENGAGEMENT

Community Engagement events are the most common type of community initiative, as they encompass art, sports, food, wellness, and entertainment. These gatherings generally occur year-round and are not necessarily contingent on current events or politics, but they can incorporate both when warranted. Community Engagement events are essentially recreational affairs that reflect the interests of a given community. As such, they happen perpetually across the globe and among all walks of life.

Despite being recreational, Community Engagement events are just as important as Preparedness and Rapid Response events. They provide an outlet for socialization and collaboration, they serve as good practice for mass mobilizing and organizing, and they empower communities. Learning to effectively plan Community Engagement events will help organizers coordinate other events that may have a narrower appeal.

Community Engagement initiatives include: **Art & Music, Sporting/Gaming & Fitness, Self Care & Wellness, and Parties & Pop-ups**.

- **Art & Music** events are shows, performances, galleries, and exhibits meant to bring people together through art. Karaoke, open mics, visual exhibits, showcases, concerts, recitals, stand-up comedy, movie nights, plays, drag shows, burlesque, dances, book clubs, writing workshops, and rap battles would all fall into this category. The possibilities are endless.

- **Sporting/Gaming & Fitness** events include basketball and football tournaments, exercise and self-defense classes, aerobic classes, yoga, billiards, hiking, video game and arcade days, board & card games, puzzles, field days, relay races and marathons.

- **Self-Care & Wellness** events include health and wellness retreats, spiritual retreats, sound baths, support groups & self-help groups, "pampering" events (hair, nails etc.), and prayer and/or meditation events.

- **Parties & Pop-Ups** include community meals, cookouts, house parties, block parties, parades, motorcades, festivals, youth engagement events, back-to-school events, and 700 people smoking weed in front of a police station.

Communities that don't engage socially are at a disadvantage when mass mobilizing and coordinating high-stakes political actions.

Community Engagement events play a vital role in providing spaces for individuals to interact and network in their personal and organizational lives. They are scrimmages for the Revolution, so always bear in mind the saying, "If it's not accessible to the poor it's neither radical nor revolutionary."

~~~

Once your team has decided to coordinate a public event, it's time to make a flyer. Frequently, flyers serve as the second-most effective means of promoting a community initiative, right behind word-of-mouth.

Making a flyer early on can help shape the vision for an event and make the idea more tangible to the organizers and the community at large. A flyer doesn't necessarily have to be circulated as soon as it's created—in fact, sharing one too early can negatively impact participation—but drafting an early concept can help the endeavor come to life. (Obvious Disclaimer: Flyers are for events that can be publicly promoted. You wouldn't make a flyer for a covert direct action or a criminal act.)

Unfortunately, however, event flyers are far too often inaccessible or lacking in critical information. Naturally, I've got a checklist to rectify this issue. Enjoy.

A flyer for an event held in 2022

How to Make an Accessible Event Flyer

1. **Make it clear.** Ensure all the vital info (date, time, and place) is depicted in a large, clear font. People shouldn't need a magnifying glass to know when and where an event is taking place.

2. **Note the full date, including day of the week (and year when possible).** Example: "Friday, March 13th, 2026." If someone has to refer to a calendar to figure out what day of the week an event is occurring, that's a problem. Flyers are supposed to _remove_ obstacles to attendance, not add them. For virtual events, be sure to include time zones: "5 p.m. EST," etc.

3. **Note the EXACT address.** If there's no exact address, make one up. An exact address is something that can be entered into a GPS to get people there. If you're struggling, go to Google Maps and figure it out. You can't just say, "Meet me at the bridge downtown" and automatically expect people in the community to understand. This is vital.

4. **Answer these questions: Who, What, When, Where, Why, and Cost.** Even if you don't spell out all the answers explicitly, a good flyer should provide insight into these questions. Who is coordinating this event? What type of event is it? When is this event occurring? Where is it occurring? Why is it occurring? And what do I need to bring to participate?

5. **Include contact info (if applicable).** This can be as basic as a hashtag or as detailed as a phone number and email. Be sure not to incriminate yourself, however. Contact information is important so community members can reach out with questions or concerns about the event.

6. **Design flyers vertically, not horizontally.** A 4:5 aspect ratio is usually best. Vertical flyers fit on phone screens better, making text more legible. They're also easier to print and share across social media. Square flyers are weird.

7. **Cater to newbies.** Try to make flyers like they're for somebody who knows nothing, or has never attended a similar event. Because that's the goal, right?—to bring new people into the fold and build community? Describe or convey the event so people know exactly what it is.

8. **Include accessibility information.** Is there seating? Wheelchair access? Sign language interpretation? Childcare? What's the terrain like? Is there a rain date? People can use this information to determine if an event is accessible to their personal needs. The more accessible an event is, the more people will attend.

9. **Try to stand out.** Don't be afraid to be bold or creative. There are lots of initiatives happening, so what makes yours different? Keep in mind we're

competing with mass budgets and state propaganda. Our creativity is often our best means of attracting new people.

10. **Find printers and designers.** Start asking around to see who dabbles in graphic design. Keep a running list of volunteers who can assist with creating event flyers. Encourage and promote this skill amongst comrades. Conduct a local survey to see who has access to copiers at their jobs so event flyers can be printed for distribution around the community. Not everyone has access to social media. When feasible, printed flyers will help get the word out. If you don't have the resources to coordinate a dedicated street team, drop stacks of flyers in local community hubs— like stores, shops, libraries, and salons.

XI

WE KEEP US SAFE
EVENT SAFETY REFERENCE GUIDE

In my free time (lol), I like to facilitate Bystander Intervention and Safety Team trainings.

Bystander Interventions are for everyday occurrences in our communities that may require community attention to mitigate harm, and Safety Team trainings (formerly Event Marshal trainings) are for addressing harm that may occur during an event, protest, or direct action. Both of these curriculums are geared towards community interdependence and self-reliance, and should be afforded time, attention, and practice to maximize safety.

There is no way to read a document about bystander intervention or event safety and have a solid grasp on what to do in the event of an emergency in your community. I strongly encourage individuals and groups to seek out in-depth, in-person courses on this material, as it can literally be the difference between life and death. (In fact, if you shoot me an email and a plane ticket I'd more than likely be willing to help facilitate a training in your area.)

That being said, I've developed a curriculum for Safety Team trainings, which I distribute as a quick reference to those who attend my in-person course. It's a living document that is available for free online and also in the following pages.

Safety Teams are not meant to provide a false sense of security for event attendees, as often the circumstances that lead to harm at an event are well beyond anyone's control. But over the years I've acquired a wealth of experience in coordinating public events and large gatherings across the Northeastern region of the United States, and I've witnessed many of the perils. More often than not, the biggest dangers we face during protests and rallies are **dehydration** and **pedestrians being struck by vehicles**. Both are generally preventable incidents. So, if you take nothing else from this chapter, let it be a newfound appreciation for having ample water and crossing guards at your events.

But if you're considering expanding your event portfolio, community safety should always be at the top of your list of priorities, and this chapter is meant to help you plan ahead.

In recent years, I've shifted the language from "event marshal" to "safety team member (STM)" or the less formal "steward," because "marshal" suggests rank or authority, and also reminds me of Eminem—who I hate.

Safety Team Members (STMs) are not authority figures and are not intended to control the crowd at an event, action, or protest. I also reject the commonly-held belief that they must serve as liaisons between the police and organizers during an action. Police Liaison is a separate role that I personally think does more harm than good, but I'll save that rant for another day.

As previously noted, STMs or stewards are volunteers assigned at demonstrations, rallies, or protests to help mitigate and contain harm within the circumstances of a given action. STMs prioritize the wellbeing of the most vulnerable, but are not replacements for medics—both are needed. Additionally, STMs do not enforce laws or protect property. They serve as the eyes and ears of an action. They should be identifiable to attendees and can work in teams or individually.

Some STM duties may include:
✓ Establishing the perimeter at an event
✓ Monitoring police movements
✓ Providing direction or assistance to attendees
✓ General traffic safety
✓ Maintaining accessibility of entrance and exit points
✓ Relaying anomalies to event organizers
✓ Communicating information to the crowd
✓ Overseeing evacuations
✓ And isolating/removing agitators or otherwise unsafe individuals when necessary and feasible.

STMs and stewards are essentially participants who have a general idea of how an event or action is intended to unfold, and do what they can to address harm that may occur in the process. That's it.

We are not cops. We are not chaperones. We are not crowd control. We do not interfere with the will of participants, so long as attendees are not being put in harm's way.

There have been several mass shootings recently where bystanders, good Samaritans, armed law enforcement, and armed civilians were on the scene before, during, and after the attack—and the shooting still occurred. STMs would likely not fare any better or worse at neutralizing an active shooter. There are societal threats and dangers STMs cannot prevent, but—like medics— we still seek to mitigate the resulting harm to the best of our ability.

STMs are an important part of any large, pre-planned event, protest, or action. However, I can say with confidence that MOST community events or protests don't have a dedicated Safety Team. The absence of a Safety Team doesn't mean events should not occur. But if your community has the resources and volunteers necessary to facilitate Safety Team trainings, they can be invaluable for your organizing efforts.

After every Safety Team Training, new trainees are added to a local mailing list and group chat so they can be deployed when necessary for upcoming events. Having a pool of pre-trained STMs is one way to increase communal safety, so it's an undertaking well worth pursuing.

Below is the quick reference guide I utilize when conducting Safety Team trainings in my community. It is a living document that is regularly updated as new situations arise. Feel free to use and modify as needed.

SAFETY TEAM QUICK REFERENCE GUIDE (WINTER 2025)

What is a Safety Team Member (STM)?

Demonstration STMs or stewards are volunteers assigned at demonstrations, rallies, or protests, to help ensure the safety of participants. STMs do not "police" attendees, but rather mitigate and contain harm within the circumstances of a given action. STMs should always prioritize the well-being of the most vulnerable. STMs are not a replacement for medics—both are needed.

What are core Safety Team duties?

✓ To help facilitate the action as planned
✓ To act as an information source between planners and demonstrators (be the eyes and ears of an action for organizers and participants)
✓ To help demonstrators be safe and feel safer while demonstrating
✓ To act as a buffer between police, agitators, and bystanders

What STMs do at a rally:
✓ Establish a perimeter
✓ Be aware of police and others' movements
✓ Lead chants (to help keep a crowd attentive)
✓ Intervene on behalf of participants (provide direction and assistance as needed)
✓ Make sure entry/exit points are accessible
✓ Stay calm; Keep crowd aware of what's happening
✓ Be visible; Wear an armband or vest distinguishing yourself as an STM
✓ Avoid carrying signs or otherwise making yourself immobile
✓ Focus on the safety of participants

What STMs do during a march:
✓ Front steward: lead at a slow, steady pace (we are safer together)
✓ Watch for obstructions
✓ Help facilitate civil disobedience, if any occurs (Example: redirect vehicles away from demonstrators in roadway)
✓ Block traffic at intersections
✓ Watch perimeters at all times
✓ Rear steward: make sure no one gets left behind

What to do at street intersections:
✓ STMs block or redirect traffic by forming a line across intersecting streets.
✓ WHENEVER POSSIBLE, allow vehicles an alternate route or a detour. Don't bring traffic to a standstill if you can redirect traffic instead.

✓ Keeping traffic flowing when possible will help discourage impatient drivers and road rage attacks

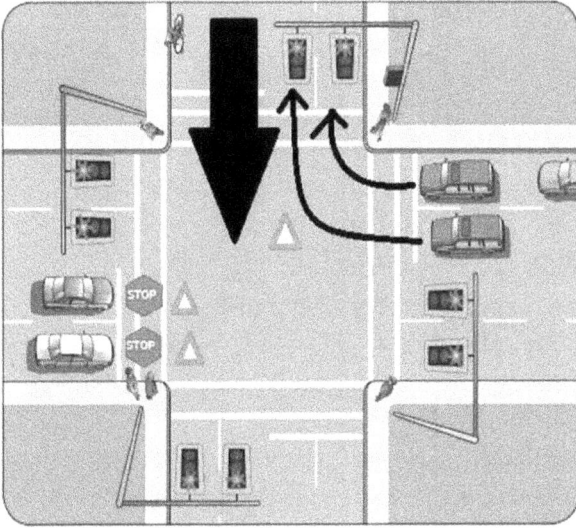

✓ In the event police block traffic, form an additional line between the police and the marchers. Don't rely solely on police to block traffic.

✓ Groups of STMs arrive at the intersection first (leap-frog other STM lines to get to the intersection).

✓ Groups of STMs wait for the red light (when cars have stopped) and quickly enter the crosswalk, facing the drivers, to stop or redirect traffic.

✓ When the march has gone by, don't dissolve until there is another red light to protect lingering STMs.

✓ When you're moving to get to the next intersection, don't run or create a panic that could lead to a stampede scenario. Hustle, don't blitz.

STM Don'ts:

✓ Don't panic.

✓ Don't act as police.

The role of police at a march:

✓ To protect property from damage

✓ To contain and disperse demonstrators; keep us from making a commotion or disturbance

How to deal with police:

✓ Ignore police "orders" whenever possible.

✓ If you must engage: Always say what you're doing is legal, and demand to know what laws are being broken. The goal is to delay and distract police or "Bluff and stall."

✓ Remember that the cops are bluffing and stalling as well. The police don't necessarily want to arrest people unless you push them or threaten their authority.

✓ If the march is large and well organized, it is difficult for the police to start arresting people.

✓ Try and remain calm whenever engaging with police.

What if police start arresting participants?

The goal is always to have zero arrests, so any decision to intervene should be made taking into account the very real dangers associated with arrest. However, it's generally safer to have mass arrests than individual arrests (more witnesses, lower charges, more community support, etc). If you decide to attempt to de-arrest someone, one method is the "Swarm and Embrace" technique. (This technique can be demonstrated to participants before and during an action).

Always remember: any and all interactions with law enforcement may result in arrest, injury, or death, and your decision to intervene on someone else's behalf may be at your own expense.

SWARM & EMBRACE TECHNIQUE:

If police attempt to arrest a demonstrator, use your body to embrace the detainee. The more people who swarm and embrace the victim, the easier it is to "de-arrest" them. This also forces the police to split their attention and focus on groups of people rather than individuals. White accomplices and those with privilege should be first in line to use their bodies to protect arrestees.

WHAT TO DO IF POLICE START ARRESTING AND/OR ABUSING ATTENDEES:

•USE YOUR BODY TO SHIELD CHILDREN AND PEOPLE OF COLOR FROM POLICE.

•USE THE "EMBRACE" TECHNIQUE IN THE EVENT OF AN ARREST. THIS INVOLVES EMBRACING THE VICTIM AND FORCING POLICE TO SPLIT THEIR ATTENTION AND RESOURCES.

•FOLLOW INDIVIDUALS WHO ARE ARRESTED SO THEY ARE NOT ISOLATED OR LOST.

•IF YOU CANNOT RISK ARREST OR INJURY, STEP ASIDE AND FILM POLICE ACTIONS. DO NOT FOCUS YOUR FOOTAGE ON THE VICTIM. FOCUS ON POLICE.

ALWAYS BE AWARE THAT ANY AND ALL INTERACTIONS WITH POLICE MAY RESULT IN ARREST, INJURY, OR DEATH, AND YOUR DECISION TO INTERVENE MAY BE AT YOUR OWN EXPENSE.

Once again (because this is important), the goal is to have *zero arrests*. But if police start abducting people, it's better to sustain mass arrests to reduce the severity of charges and increase the likelihood of dismissals. The Swarm and Embrace technique involves exposing your body to law enforcement officers, and as with all police contact, can result in injury or death. People who employ this technique should be made aware of the potential risks.

If arrests occur, follow those who are arrested so they are not lost or isolated. Get their names when possible.

Film the police when arrests are happening. Focus footage on police actions, not the actions of the victim(s). Afterwards, reach out to organizers or victims to see if they can make use of the footage for their defense.

Dealing with agitators/hecklers/counter-protestors (Identify, Ignore, Isolate, Expel):

✓ **Identify** - Be observant in identifying people who may be present to cause harm to participants. When an agitator is spotted, identify them to other stewards and alert the crowd if necessary. "This person is not with us! Be aware of this person!"

✓ **Ignore** - Most agitators and counter-protestors can be ignored if they don't pose an immediate threat and are instead standing off to the side heckling the crowd. Ignore these people unless they become a direct threat.

✓ **Isolate** - If an unarmed agitator is causing a disturbance or becoming a direct threat, STMs should isolate the individual and attempt to separate them from the larger crowd. Yell "MARSHAL!" to get more assistance in isolating agitators or serving as a buffer between agitators and participants.

✓ **Expel** - Removing an unarmed agitator is done more safely in teams—with the smallest STM walking backward (arms extended) into the agitator while larger STMs guide the direction of the extraction and protect the STM walking backward. When done correctly, this looks very similar to the "boxing out" technique used in basketball. Expelling in this manner is a de-escalation technique, and takes practice to get right. Expelling an agitator is a last-resort measure.

What if an agitator is armed?

This has to be handled on a case-by-case basis, but the goal remains keeping vulnerable people safe. Alert the crowd to the threat, and do what must be done to ensure your safety, and the safety of others. Overwhelmingly this means getting yourself and others *away* from the threat.

In case of a medical emergency: One STM remains with the injured person while another gets a medic and/or calls 911.

What if an abuser is present?

You may be informed by an attendee that an abuser is present in the crowd, and their presence is harmful.

Ask the survivor what they need: Would they like a Safety Team Member to stay by their side? Would they like us to keep an eye on the abuser?

In some instances, it may be requested that the abuser be removed from the event. This would need to be handled on a case-by-case basis. What is the abuse in question? Is it ongoing? Who is most at risk by the abuser's presence, and how severe is the risk? A local pedophile at a park event, for example, poses a different immediate risk than a man who financially abused his ex-partner. Assess the risks, harm, and possible alternatives before escalating the situation through isolation and removal.

Communication:

✓ Use hand signals, walkies, verbal commands, and megaphones to communicate with other STMs and the crowd as needed.

✓ Use walkies as minimally as possible, as the channels are not secure.

✓ Make sure walkies and bullhorns are fully charged before events.

✓ Predetermine the channel or frequency your team will be using for the action. Different teams can use different channels if necessary.

✓ Use encrypted messaging apps for organizational work, but assume all messages sent or received on your personal devices can be retrieved by authorities.

Contingency routes/plans:

Have a backup destination established in case an emergency or obstruction occurs that forces the action to re-group elsewhere. Have pre-determined evacuation routes for making a speedy exit.

Disperse QUICKLY and together:

Encourage people to leave in groups, quickly and collectively. You don't want stragglers to be harmed by agitators or picked up by police after the action.

Safety Team Member uniform:

✓ Sturdy, comfortable shoes!
✓ Reflective arm tape or reflective vest
✓ Extra t-shirt or fabric cloth (for stopping bleeding, breathing through if you don't have a gas mask, or wiping chemicals from skin, etc - very handy)
✓ Bottle(s) of water
✓ Helmet, knee pads, and/or goggles if it's that type of party

REMINDER: This reference document is not comprehensive, and should not be used as a replacement for in-person trainings and/or teach-ins.

TOOLS OF THE TRADE
ORGANIZING SUPPLY CHECKLIST

Here's a list of items that will help your organizing efforts. None of these items are a necessity, but if you're going to do the work, you may as well try and acquire the tools of the trade.

1. **Collapsible Wagon:** A wagon's at the top of this list because you'll need it to haul around all the other stuff. They're great for marches, rallies, trainings, and protests. And in a pinch, you can use one to shield yourself from pepper spray. Don't ask me how I know.

2. **Folding Tables:** Portability is the name of the game. Folding tables allow you to have events anywhere. However many you think you'll need, double it.

3. **Bullhorn/Megaphone:** I go through at least two bullhorns a year. Usually, they get confiscated by the police or "borrowed" by other organizers. Keep them handy. 50 watt minimum.

4. **Rechargeable Battery for Bullhorn:** This is a must-have item if you don't want to spend the rest of your life stealing C batteries. Get the ones that plug directly into the wall and thank me later.

5. **Karaoke Speaker or Portable PA System:** A good portable speaker system will allow you to play music at events and also speak clearly to a crowd. Keep in mind, you get what you pay for.

6. **Portable Power Station/Power Bank:** You may be noticing a trend here. Lots of community organizing happens on the road. Having your own power supply prevents you from being tethered to one location or relying on city governments to turn power on in public spaces. Shoot for at least 50000mAh battery capacity. Bonus points if it has solar charging capabilities.

7. **A Really Good First Aid Kit:** You're gonna need at least one well-packed trauma kit (sometimes called IFAKs). The more medics you have, the more kits you'll need. Don't just grab a basic first aid kit from the pharmacy. You want one that can help patch up a gunshot wound.

8. **Power Inverter for Car:** These are handy devices that turn every car into a generator. Never leave home without it. 800 watt minimum.

9. **Gas Powered Generator (Preferably an Inverter Generator):** These are great for emergencies and large events that will require an extended power supply. Check your local used marketplaces for cheap deals.

10. **Pop-Up Canopy Tents:** Pop-up tents are a must. Do yourself a favor and get the ones that say "commercial" or "industrial" grade; they last much longer. Also, rectangular tents are more versatile than squares. Take my word for it.

11. **Walkie-Talkies:** You're gonna want easy-to-use, rechargeable walkie-talkies. Most will have up to a two-mile range. Buy a six-pack that comes with a multi-unit charger so you're not using a half dozen outlets in your house. Keep these charged at all times.

12. **Miscellaneous Items:** Folding chairs, helmets & knee pads, duct tape, zip ties, contractor bags, a large cooler, a thermal beverage cooler, a digital VPN, heavy-duty extension cords, an excellent surge protector, and guns. Lots of guns.

XIII

ALL MONEY AIN'T GOOD MONEY
FUNDRAISING & REPARATIONS

Once upon a time, a local Black woman and friend lost her vehicle following an unfortunate collision. Thankfully, nobody was injured in the crash, but the car was damaged beyond repair.

I, along with some comrades, decided to launch a fundraiser on the woman's behalf in the hopes of purchasing a replacement vehicle. It was a long shot, but we knew the loss of transportation would significantly impact her family and also the community as a whole.

Before long, donations started rolling in. Among them was an offer from a community member willing to donate a working vehicle in exchange for whatever amount we were able to raise. The donor was an avid supporter and follower of the work being done within my organizing community. She trusted that the donation would go to good use and was willing to take a financial loss if it meant helping our efforts. Within 24 hours my friend was back on the road.

Over the years, I've collected all sorts of items from generous donors seeking to help marginalized people—from washing machines, to tables, chairs, bed frames and mattresses, couches, clothing, and even recreational drugs. Overwhelmingly, I distribute these resources into the community to those in need, but occasionally *I'm* the person in need, or I will commandeer household items for struggling family members and friends. To date, I've also crowdsourced roughly $250,000 in cash reparations and donations for Black women on my radar. I intentionally do this using the direct payment links of recipients so as to limit any cash passing through my possession.

In addition to direct giving campaigns for individuals, it's also common for groups to fundraise specific resources for an organization, upcoming event, or the community as a whole. My collective has received donations for everything from tents to sound systems, bullhorns, tools, toys, and school supplies. Internal discussions are occasionally held about the ethics of directing resources towards things like bicycle chains and Halloween candy, when many children in our city are actively without food and shelter. But since no amount of fundraising could ever fill the chasm of suffering imposed by capitalism, we try to focus on collective empowerment and systemic solutions, rather than feebly attempting to meet the basic needs of every individual.

Still, fundraising is 90% of my motivation behind maintaining a social media presence—not because I think it will bring about systemic change, but because I realized long ago that sometimes the difference between staying afloat and drowning is a few hundred bucks. And since Black women do a disproportionate amount of community labor, it seemed prudent to have a mechanism in place to redistribute resources to them when possible.

My online platform is relatively small but still has a reputation for being a helpful independent fundraising tool for Black women. Donors willingly offer money and other items to campaigns I highlight because of trust I've built with the community while fostering a culture of direct giving. And there are many, *many* pages like mine with even better success rates for crowdfunding resources for individuals. Some of them have raised millions of dollars in recent years.

Contrary to popular belief, community organizing is not entirely selfless work. Aside from being extremely rewarding emotionally and socially, organizing can be financially lucrative. It's not uncommon for organizers to get addicted to the perks associated with advocacy once they've established themselves as trustworthy and effective. Combine that with the fact that many organizers are also extremely vulnerable members of society trying to survive capitalism, and you have the perfect recipe for financial abuse.

If organizers aren't withholding cash donations for personal gain, they're still very likely to gatekeep resources—intentionally or unintentionally—by picking and choosing who gets access to what. For every successful fundraising campaign I promote, there are a dozen requests that go unanswered. My friend got first dibs on a free car simply because I chose to highlight her need. How is that fair?

The answer is, "It's not." And this is where things get messy.

You may have heard the phrase, "There's no ethical consumption under capitalism." I've come to believe that this rule extends beyond mere consumption and applies to virtually all wealth redistribution. Ideally, the goal is to prioritize the well-being of the "most marginalized," but that ever-changing demographic is not always obvious nor accessible.

If we were to second-guess every charitable transaction, funds would sit idle indefinitely. "Scarcity mindset" often creates a bottleneck of resources as donors and orgs try to determine the perceived *worthiness* of potential recipients through vetting and eligibility requirements. But once we accept that all wealth exchanges under capitalism are inherently unethical and biased, we can be more intentional about acquiring and distributing resources—while also shedding the false notion that there's a perfectly fair way to do either.

I'm often asked, "Why fundraise or distribute reparations at all? Wouldn't it be more effective to prioritize grants and other resources available to nonprofits from private foundations or the government?" The short answer is "No." The longer answer is spelled out in the opening passages of *Philanthropy and Cultural Imperialism* by Professor Robert Arnove. He writes:

> Foundations have a corrosive influence on a democratic society; they represent relatively unregulated and unaccountable concentrations of power and wealth which buy talent, promote causes, and, in effect, establish an agenda of what merits society's attention. They serve as 'cooling-out' agencies, delaying and preventing more radical, structural change. They help maintain an economic and political order, international in scope, which benefits the ruling-class interests of philanthropists [...] – a system which has worked against the interests of minorities, the working class, and Third World peoples.

Grants primarily function as a way for powerful entities to gatekeep and distribute resources at their discretion—which intrinsically aligns with the interests of the ruling class as opposed to radical and transformative agendas. To make matters worse, the resources being distributed through grant foundations are overwhelmingly a product of capitalist exploitation of the working class. As noted by Andrea Smith in *The Revolution Will not be Funded: Beyond the Non-Profit Industrial Complex*:

When wealthy people create foundations, they're exempt from paying taxes on their wealth. Thus foundations essentially rob the public of monies that should be owed to them and give back very little of what is taken in lost taxes. In addition, their funds are derived from profits resulting from the exploitation of labor. That is, corporations become rich by exploiting their workers. Corporate profits are then put into foundations in order to provide "relief" to workers that are the result of corporate practices in the first place.

This theme of performative, incremental faux-relief is pervasive under capitalism. It's the reason police don't actually work towards ending crime because they'd be out of a job if they succeeded. It's why Walmart's wages are so low that their employees are eligible for food stamps, which are then spent right back at Walmart. The millionaires and billionaires funding grant foundations create the problems these grants pretend to address through nonprofits, rather than just curtailing their own greed.

To complicate matters further, nonprofits have to compete with each other for grant money in order to keep operating. That means initiatives are often crafted to meet grant requirements, rather than the needs of the community. Government grants are even more stringent, meticulously tracking every dollar spent and by whom. As such, radical events and undertakings that truly challenge the status quo do not qualify for financial aid.

Additionally, the grant application process is often time-consuming and tedious, draining vital energy and resources that are already spread thin among community organizations.

That's not to say there aren't occasionally opportunities to "launder" grant money and redirect it towards radical initiatives, but those opportunities are exceedingly rare and often come with additional stipulations. In other words, "grant money got strings attached." But, naturally, fundraising also comes with its own pitfalls.

There's a content creator by the name of Shaun King who used his enormous online platform and status as a career activist to become a millionaire. He's regularly accused of "grifting" funds and conning vulnerable people out of resources through fundraisers and donor campaigns. In 2021, he was selling plain white hoodies on his website for $150 each. When I started online fundraising many years ago, I decided to do the opposite of everything Shaun King did, and so far it's worked out.

As such, I've compiled a set of guidelines to assist in collecting and re-distributing resources in ways that prioritize the most marginalized and reduce the likelihood of fraud or theft. Those guidelines can be found in the following pages. I'm still occasionally accused of mismanaging funds, but I very rarely receive funds to manage at all; and, for what it's worth, I've never sold a shirt for more than 20 bucks.

FUNDRAISING GUIDELINES:

1. **Fundraise for the most marginalized.**
   Other than fundraising for organizational purchases and community initiatives, you should always prioritize the most marginalized. It is for this reason I don't fundraise for men or white people. I focus on Black women and children, making exceptions only for extenuating circumstances. This is because those with the least amount of privilege are the least likely to have their needs met. Generally, there will always be someone MORE marginalized along intersections, but it's a good rule of thumb to start with Black women.

2. **Target the most privileged donors.**
   Have you ever heard the anecdote that poor customers tip servers more than wealthy customers? Well, this is also true of fundraising. To try and alleviate the impulse of marginalized people to contribute their last to a comrade in need, target fundraisers towards people with privilege— specifically cis-men and non-Black individuals. Those with the most should be giving the most.

3. **Promote a culture of direct giving.**
   Start using the word "reparations" more. Delete people from your social media who scoff at direct giving. Thank people who donate to create a positive feedback loop. Provide results and updates on campaign milestones and goal completions. The idea is to cultivate an environment that normalizes

supporting people based on their needs rather than their abilities.

4. **Fundraise for others rather than yourself.**
Fundraising for yourself or personal initiatives can be off-putting to donors, who may feel the campaign is a self-serving cash grab. Raising funds for other people or for community initiatives generally yields better results. Organizations, however, should try to avoid fundraising for individuals, as you will undoubtedly be accused of playing favorites.

5. **Don't hoard funds.**
There are very few reasons to sit on cash and resources rather than immediately dispersing them to the community. Bail funds are sometimes necessary, but generally speaking, get cash in and then get it out quickly. The longer you sit on funds, the higher the chance for accusations of mismanagement and opportunities for theft.

6. **In fact, don't even collect funds at all.**
If you are fundraising online for an individual, make a habit of using their own payment links or the links of people they trust. The less cash going through you as an intermediary, the better.

7. **Prioritize "stuff" over cash.**
Cash isn't always king. Donors are more likely to contribute items directly when given the option. This way they know for certain where their money

is going. Create a wishlist or registry online, and promote that whenever possible. Make direct asks for items and utilities rather than cash donations. If we can bypass commerce through trading, swapping, and giving away physical resources, it will help subvert capitalism while also helping those in need.

8. **Work first, fundraise later.**
Nothing motivates people like results. Start organizing NOW with the resources you have. Then when people see the work being done, use that opportunity to ask them to support the continuation of that work. If you ask people for money and resources to get started, you've already set yourself up for failure. Whatever resources are at your disposal are enough to get started. The more you accomplish with those resources, the more people will want to pitch in to keep the momentum going.

9. **Don't exhaust your donors.**
Although fundraising is largely why I keep an online presence, most of my content is not related to fundraising. Donor fatigue is real. The goal is to be insightful, informative, and (dare I say) humorous to engage your followers. Fundraisers should be sprinkled in sparingly. If you have too many recurring asks, none of them will get filled. But if you are intentional about your reach and capacity when crowdfunding, you will generally yield better results. That means saying "no" to fundraising requests far more often than you say "yes."

10. Make it easy!

When fundraising online, include multiple payment links representing the various online and app-based payment options. The more links, the broader your donor base. If you're asking people to mail a certified check to your P.O. box, it's unlikely your campaign will get much traction. At community events, have a simple reparations "tip" jar where people can toss in cash. The more obstacles in place to collect donations, the fewer donations you'll receive. Make donating as easy as possible.

Bear in mind, following these guidelines doesn't guarantee success in fundraising, because there are so many factors at play. My early online fundraisers would sometimes have one single contributor. During peak periods of modern resistance, like the early days of Black Lives Matter and the 2020 Uprisings, money was rolling in like never before. Things like the cost of groceries and the unemployment rate impact the amount of resources available to be collected and redistributed from donors.

The important thing to remember is that our most valuable resource as a community is not money, but people. Work with what you got.

XIV

DON'T KILL YOURSELF
RESPECTING YOUR CAPACITY BY SAYING "NO"

TW: Detailed descriptions of su*cide

~~~

One evening, when I was 16 years old, my siblings and I left home for a few hours at our mother's request. Upon returning, we found her convulsing in bed.

She was surrounded by empty pill bottles and actively foaming at the mouth. Her skin was ashen and her lips were nearly blue. Both of her arms were tied to the bed frame.

By the time the medics arrived, our mother had stopped moving. They untied her and began administering aid. We watched in silent horror.

Later, at the hospital, the doctor told us she would likely not survive the night, and we should begin preparing for the worst.

But my mother didn't die.

They pumped her full of charcoal to help absorb the drugs. She stabilized over the next 48 hours but remained unconscious for several days. I was later told she survived, in part, because of her high body weight, as the cocktail of drugs would likely have killed a smaller person.

When my mother finally regained consciousness, I couldn't help but ask why she'd tied her arms to the bed. She told me it was so she wouldn't injure herself and get blood everywhere, which seemed like an odd concern for someone taking their life. I later deduced it was actually so she couldn't call for help or induce vomiting had she changed her mind—a detail I still find jarring. This obviously wasn't her first attempt.

Although my mother survived the overdose that night, the drugs did extensive damage to her liver and kidneys. She also sustained permanent nerve damage, which significantly impaired her mobility and coordination. Before this incident, she had been living with depression for several years. Afterward, she developed an entirely new set of physical disabilities and ailments to accompany her ongoing mental health issues. Ironically, however, her new condition left her eligible for various disability benefits and social services of which she was previously exempt. And that help, as it turns out, made a big impact.

For a time, her mental health improved almost as quickly as her physical health deteriorated. Soon, she was smiling and laughing again. She was even able to receive and provide love. But she now required the use of a wheelchair to move about. Eventually, regular dialysis treatments were necessary to remove toxins and waste from her blood.

My mother began what would ultimately be the final chapter of her life. She was living and she was dying— as we all are. This period lasted for over a decade. She would joke that this must be the slowest suicide in history.

My mother was a month shy of her 52nd birthday when she finally succumbed to renal failure one frigid February evening.

In the years immediately following her death, my mental health took a nose-dive. Community organizing provided me with an outlet to distract myself from my own mental health woes, but like most distractions, it eventually developed into a coping mechanism. My mother was an artist and activist in her own right, and I felt closer to her when I was engaged in those endeavors. A part of me became obsessed. It took years of therapy for me to come to grips with the ways I was processing my grief and past trauma, all while simultaneously dealing with the ongoing pressures of daily life.

In February 2017, exactly five years after my mother's death, I was admitted to the Inpatient Mental Health Unit at Samaritan Hospital in Troy, New York, after a failed suicide attempt. A few months later, a good friend of mine, whom I greatly admired, took her own life in a cemetery in Upstate New York. Shortly thereafter, three more friends and acquaintances completed suicide—one after the other—within a four-year span. We were all artists and community organizers.

In organizing spaces, suicide is so prevalent that it can be overlooked and ignored until it's too late. Those who do confront it head-on are often accused of exploiting tragedy for attention or recognition. We use buzzwords like "burnout" and "self-care" without actually stopping long enough to address the driving forces behind our suffering. And, yes, organizing compulsively can be a form of self-harm stopping us from doing the internal work necessary to prioritize our wellbeing (especially since most of us find it easier to advocate for others than for ourselves). But organizing can also be a form of healing, providing us with a connection to community and a sense of camaraderie needed to find hope in an otherwise bleak world.

Telling organizers to "take a break" isn't always helpful or plausible, especially when organizing is frequently the only light in our lives. Many of my friends completed suicide while "on a break" from organizing. I miss them dearly and wish we'd had mechanisms in place to address their pain before they transitioned from this life. I liken each suicide attempt to a direct action taken out of desperation when all other avenues fail, and I believe it's our duty as survivors and organizers to preserve life and end suffering with a true sense of urgency.

As blogger and activist Vu Le of *Rooted in Vibrant Communities Seattle* writes:

> Suicide among nonprofit professionals and social justice activists needs to be recognized as an issue. Many of us entered this line of work because we have dealt with trauma in our own lives. We have seen and felt firsthand the effects of injustice, and it drove many of us into the field. Our traumas make us more empathetic and often more effective. But this empathy and drive can also be too much, as we are constantly re-traumatized by seeing others being beaten down by unjust systems as we do the work each day.

I'm now, at the time of this writing, the same age my mother was when I found her tied to that mattress many years ago. And like her, I'm still struggling with mental health issues. In fact, the book you're currently reading originally began as a suicide note, but I got distracted somewhere along the way. Thank you for indulging me.

I've now begun the process of shifting into a new phase of organizing in order to sustain myself mentally and physically. And also to make way for the next generation of organizers, and the new ideas and courageousness they bring with them. Organizing has saved my life more times than I can count, and I remain grateful, but I also recognize a need for change. Some may say I've finally burnt out, but I don't see it that way.

If we organize effectively and efficiently for a few years and get "burnt out," that's arguably better than cautiously threading the needle for decades at a time and getting nothing accomplished.

I know career activists who've been organizing since the 1970s and haven't done much aside from voter registration. And I know folks who've pushed it hard for one summer and managed to inspire an entire community.

We don't call it burnout when someone finishes college or retires from competitive sports and then refocuses their efforts. We say they accomplished a goal. They completed a mission. Burnout only occurs when we're consistently exceeding our mental, physical, and emotional capacities—which differ for everyone.

When I look back at the challenges faced and accomplishments achieved over the past several years of my life, I'm aware of what I have sacrificed, but also what I have gained. I no longer see liberation as an end goal, because I have already been liberated through the Struggle. Each of us is on an interconnected path that we cannot separate ourselves from, as our humanity is intrinsically and eternally connected. Even our untimely death will not remove us from this path.

To anyone reading this who feels they are drowning, I want to assure you that things will get better. Yes, even as the world around us worsens, we will have good days and bad. It's not on us as individuals to save the world. Many of us are struggling to save ourselves. You are not alone. Practice saying, "I'm at capacity." Practice saying, "I need help." Practice saying, "No." A major part of organizing is checking in with ourselves to see how well we are functioning so that we can be healthy and sustained in our everyday lives. Each of us matters as individuals, regardless of what we contribute to the collective, but if we are not prioritizing ourselves, we're also putting the community at risk.

By some measures, I'm considered a highly productive, highly visible organizer, but most aren't privy to the boundaries I've put in place to respect my own capacity. Spectators may see things I do, but they don't see the many instances where I decline participation or step back because I know my own limits. We shouldn't compare ourselves to others while engaging in movement work, because we are all at different parts of our journey. Do what you are willing and capable of, and don't allow yourself to be pressured or guilted into doing anything more OR less.

If organizing brings you peace or a sense of purpose, by all means, do so with a sense of duty and commitment that sustains you. But do so at your own pace. Slow down when necessary, and know when it's time to kick things into high gear.

If you lack the instincts or perspective to put yourself first, simply because you are entitled to, do it for the community. Do it for your family and friends. Do it for your children. Do it for your pets. It's OK to neglect responsibilities if it means saving your life, because if you die your responsibilities will still be neglected, only now you'll be gone.

I have seen first-hand what happens when one of us succumbs to pain and despair. The holes we leave behind are never filled, and the ripples of grief turn into unrelenting waves. Be kind to yourself, always.

Forgive yourself.

XV

ELECTION REJECTION
THE MYTH OF ELECTORAL HARM REDUCTION

Abraham Lincoln famously said in regard to social victories, "Not bloody bullets, but peaceful ballots only, are necessary." A few years later he was shot in the back of the head.

Lincoln, like many, learned the hard way that changing society has little to do with casting ballots, and everything to do with direct action. Still, electoral politics retain a proverbial chokehold on the vast majority of Americans on both sides of the political spectrum, desperate for change.

I don't know many Leftists who didn't first get involved in politics because a particular political figure caught their attention and perhaps inspired hope. From Lincoln to Kennedy, to the other Kennedy; to Clinton, to Obama, to the other Clinton—politicians are often a gateway drug to radicalization, even if unintentionally. So, while electoral campaigns aren't what we usually think of when discussing radical community organizing, for many organizers they are our first introduction to political engagement—for better or for worse. As a result, the significance of voting may be the most controversial topic among those who consider themselves left of liberal... and that's saying something.

Personally, I was all but done with elections when Barack Obama announced his presidential bid in 2007, but the temptation of a Black candidate with an African name-calling for universal healthcare, withdrawal from Iraq, and codified abortion rights sounded too good to pass up. Additionally, the propaganda around Obama was like nothing I'd experienced before. His likeness was everywhere. His rallies regularly topped 100,000 attendees. Rappers were shouting him out on street records and Billboard hits. For the first time in my life, I saw other Black men excited to register and cast their votes, and I reluctantly counted myself among them.

So when Obama ended up being another smooth-talking fascist, like so many of his predecessors, I vowed to never be duped by another celebrity politician promising radical change again. Propaganda had won out for the last time. Bernie Sanders could have dropped an album with Kendrick Lamar and I still wouldn't have voted for him. And the more I came to understand the true purpose of electoral politics and the ways voting was designed to uphold capitalism—including in local elections—the more I began embracing other more radical means of bringing about systemic change.

Still, I make it a point not to actively discourage people from participating in our current electoral system, because I see value in voters becoming disenfranchised on their own, like I did. But I do take issue with entities that seem determined to shame and belittle people (especially marginalized folks) for choosing to abstain from voting.

Society has been so indoctrinated by the idea that casting a ballot is the most effective and viable way to bring about change that it's become one of the more challenging notions to unlearn. We're told in grade school that voting is not only our civic duty, but that our ancestors *literally died* for our right to vote. And while voting as a concept isn't inherently harmful, the current electoral system in the United States is designed to render participation antithetical to social progress and stifling to meaningful change.

This is, in part, because presidential elections are essentially rigged, and that's not even a radical notion. According to a 2024 Pew Research poll, "More than six-in-ten Americans (63%) would prefer to see the winner of the presidential election be the person who wins the most votes." Only 35% of Americans favor retaining the Electoral College. Under the Electoral College, a handful of swing states regularly dictate the outcome of every presidential election, regardless of who wins the popular vote. If you live in any of the other 43 states, your vote for president is essentially moot. But it could be worse, since nearly 4 million American citizens currently living in U.S. territories (like Puerto Rico, Guam, and the Virgin Islands) aren't even allowed to vote for president.

Furthermore, a now-infamous study conducted by The Center for Economic and Policy Research (CEPR) candidly states, "In the Electoral College, white votes matter more."

As Andrew Gelman, professor of statistics and political science at Columbia University, explains, "Based on the current distribution of voters of different ethnicities across states, and particularly within swing states, the Electoral College amplifies the power of white voters by a substantial amount." He adds, "Whites have 16% more power than Blacks once the Electoral College is taken into consideration, 28% more power than Latinos, and 57% more power than those who fall into the 'Other' category."

If you're thinking, "This sounds eerily similar to the Three-Fifths Compromise of 1787, under which individual slaves counted as 3/5ths of a person towards a state's total population to determine representation in Congress," you'd be correct. The voices of white Americans have *always* counted more in this country, and every time we cast a vote we're saying, "That's fine by me."

So, studies confirm the system for determining the president is blatantly racist, and the majority of Americans don't favor that system in the first place, yet most of us (66%) still willingly participate. Why?

We do this out of desperation and indoctrination. Many Americans believe there is no other viable choice outside of the electoral process. They say things like, "Until the Revolution happens, this is the best we can do." We're lectured repeatedly that if we don't vote, we're not even entitled to complain, which is a convenient way to silence marginalized voices. Truth be told, our willing participation in the system is the only reason it persists, and revolutions require a rejection of all civic engagement designed to quell dissent.

George Jackson notes this in his political memoir, *Blood In My Eye*, which was completed only days before he was killed by the state.

> When any election is held it will fortify
> rather than destroy the credibility of [those in
> power]. When we participate in an election
> to win, instead of disrupt, we're lending to its
> credibility, and destroying our own. With all
> the factors of control over the electoral process
> in the hands of the ruling class, the people's

party can always be made to seem isolated, unimportant, even extraneous. If these tactics still give the appearance of revolution to some after decades of miscarriage, we are justified in replacing them as vanguard.

Jackson argues that participation in elections is not only harmful, it's self-defeating and counter-revolutionary, and those who continue to tout voting as a revolutionary act of resistance have no business leading social movements.

It's worth noting that Jackson's stance is not synonymous with "voter apathy," which is used to describe those who simply see voting as useless or a waste of time. If voting were merely a waste of time, I'd support it. Wasting time is generally harmless. In fact, it can be fun and even radical. In a world where many insist "time is money," wasting time can even be anti-capitalist. But, tragically, voting is none of those things. Participation in the current electoral system presented to American voters is actively harmful, and it's past time we get comfortable acknowledging that fact.

When Jackson suggests constituents "disrupt" elections rather than participate, he means rejecting the illusion of choice posed by the two-party system that has always dominated American politics. This rejection can take many forms, from casting a protest vote, to voting for third party candidates who have zero shot of winning, to outright abstaining from the process. (Incidentally, my mother went into labor with me on Election Day and couldn't make it to the polls, so I've technically been disrupting electoral politics for my entire life. *Rimshot*)

The main takeaway here is that if we continue to participate, the process has no incentive to change. Disruption is the only true threat. As such, any action that exposes, discredits, impedes, or otherwise undermines the electoral process is stigmatized as naive or deviant by society, because—above all else—the system requires participation.

Americans are so indoctrinated by the idea of voting that abandoning the electoral process can feel like an overwhelming loss. It's one thing to be critical of our government and the ruling class, but it's another to accept that voting is an intricate placebo designed to uphold the status quo at the expense of the oppressed.

We may even go through the **Stages of Electoral Grief** before accepting that we've been misled by a system that was never intended to truly reflect the will of The People™. It usually goes something like this:

• **Denial:** "Voting works; we just have to keep voting and do a better job of getting young people registered and to the polls."

• **Anger:** "Anyone who doesn't vote is an enemy to the American people! Do you want [Bad Man] to win?!"

- **Bargaining:** "OK, I'll concede that national elections don't carry much weight, but LOCAL ELECTIONS are surely important. That's how we're going to improve society."

- **Depression:** "Fuck."

- **Acceptance:** "Workers of the world, unite! We have nothing to lose but our chains!"

Most people get hung up on the Bargaining Stage, because it stands to reason that if the Electoral College is unjust, local elections will result in a more representative government better suited to serve a given community. It's easy to denounce presidential candidates as power-hungry oligarchs intent on upholding the status quo, but it's more challenging to suggest our friends and peers who comprise city councils, school boards, state legislatures, and municipal offices are complicit as well. Especially when those positions are held by people who look like us.

But we need only observe Democratic cities and states to see that diverse, liberal governments don't equate to justice or even basic dignity. For starters, "Blue" cities and states are among the poorest.

The 2020 Census ranked California and Washington D.C. as the two locales with the highest poverty rates per capita, according to the Supplemental Poverty Measure (SPM), which factors in each state or district's cost of living. The top ten list included New York, Hawaii, and New Mexico, which all have overwhelmingly Democratic governments.

Additionally, as noted by Jed Kolko, the former Under Secretary of Commerce for Economic Affairs, "Even after adjusting for differences of income, liberal markets tend to have higher income inequality and worse affordability." According to data from the U.S. Department of Housing and Urban Development, the states with the highest rates of homelessness in 2023 were (in order): New York, Vermont, Oregon, California, Hawaii, Washington, Maine, and Massachusetts—all Democratic strongholds.

So while it's great that abortion access, for example, is still relatively available in these states, it's unfortunate that parents and children residing there are more likely to have to live on the streets. If this is what's passing for "harm reduction" these days, I'd say it's time to re-evaluate.

Still, some insist that Democratic states have higher rates of homelessness and poverty simply because poor people flock to these regions to reap the public benefits and social services available under their liberal leadership and progressive policies. I'd argue that claiming someone would rather suffer in New York than, say, Alabama, is a pretty low bar to serve as an example of local elections making a difference.

But if local elections are indeed the gold standard for American democracy, is this truly the best we can do? Every two to four years we're expected to vote for our most basic human rights, and if we miss a year we risk losing everything.

And what about people suffering in neighboring towns and states? Are we supposed to ignore them and just "vote local" so we don't end up like them? Don't we want ALL children safe? Don't we want reproductive rights for ALL? Don't we want human dignity, food, healthcare, and housing for ALL? Or is that just something we say while fighting for scraps of comfort and dignity afforded to those with enough privilege to keep their heads above water? Because even in the most progressive and liberal states, children go to sleep hungry, disabled people fall through the gaping holes of the system, and queer and trans folks go without housing and healthcare; all while our tax dollars fund rampant police violence instead of confronting these problems head-on. Every time we cast a vote for the status quo, we're sacrificing the most marginalized and writing them off as collateral damage because we fear it "could be worse."

Worse for *whom*?

Whether people flee to conservative states to find more affordable housing or liberal states to access reproductive healthcare, the reality remains that most Americans are faced with choosing which of their human rights they're willing to forfeit to survive. The homeless encampments popping up in America's liberal cities are increasingly destroyed by law enforcement agencies run by Black and brown police chiefs, appointed by Black and brown mayors, using budgets approved by Black and brown City Council members. Record numbers of women now hold office at federal and state levels, but even the most diverse political representation in U.S. history has only succeeded in making it more challenging to confront oppressive policies, systemic abuse, and mismanagement across the board.

In 1956, W.E.B. Dubois wrote, "Democracy has so far disappeared in the United States that no 'two evils' exist. There is but one evil party with two names, and it will be elected despite all I can do or say." That was written before Black Americans secured the right to vote, but is now more true than ever. Local elections remain entrenched in the two-party system, and diverse and progressive candidates are forced to compromise their principles and messaging if they hope to win a seat at the table.

The underlying theme here is that reform doesn't work at a local level any better than it works at a national level. Flipping states and cities Blue and tokenizing diverse candidates is ineffective in addressing social inequality because the frameworks in place are inherently designed to uphold oppressive systems. The notion that Democrats seek to end poverty and discrimination is a blatant falsehood because Democrats seek to preserve capitalism, which requires exploitation of the working class.

"The oppressed," writes Karl Marx, "are allowed once every few years to decide which particular representatives of the oppressing class are to represent and repress them." It is in this way that both major parties ensure that the back-and-forth game of politics never ends, in an effort to retain power and control of the masses.

Case in point: Since 1977, Democrats have had four opportunities to codify Roe v. Wade into law, ensuring reproductive rights for all. Yet each time they chose not to, for the express purpose of holding American voters hostage with the threat of losing abortion access. Frustratingly, this strategy continues to prove effective because voter turnout is at an all-time high.

In fact, the 2020 *and* 2024 presidential elections, respectively, had the highest voter turnout rates for ANY national elections held since 1900. And the 2018 and 2022 midterms had the highest midterm turnouts of the past 50 years. Despite persistent talk of voter apathy, voter suppression, and fear-mongering claims that voting rights are "under attack," Americans are hitting the polls like never before. Voting remains the status quo across virtually *all* demographics. Participation in the electoral process is the default position among Republicans and Democrats alike, and indeed the overwhelming majority of Americans. Yet there is outrage whenever someone even *hints* at the idea of not voting. I personally know many individuals who lie and say they voted, just so they don't get shamed and judged by their peers.

We should ask ourselves why this is happening. **When is it ever worthwhile to defend the dominant opinion so fervently?**

Those who do abstain from voting generally do so conscientiously for a number of reasons. Some abstain because the system has proven ineffective and/or detrimental to the most marginalized. "Since candidates running for office seldom represent the interests of Black and poor people," writes Assata Shakur, "Blacks and the poor don't vote." Others abstain because our government is complicit in genocides (plural) which are routinely supported by both major parties. Some simply don't have the will or energy to vote since they're too busy trying to survive under the crushing weight of capitalism. And still others abstain because they refuse to participate or lend credibility to a system that is so blatantly corrupt and discriminatory.

As such, the way to increase voter turnout amongst these groups is simply by addressing those valid concerns, not by shaming constituents into compliance. Parties and politicians who fail to meet the needs of The People™ are undeserving of our votes, even if they portray themselves as "harm reduction" candidates.

Indeed, the concept of voting as harm reduction is itself damaging to society, as noted by author and activist Rudy Preston in his 2020 piece, "Voting is Not Harm Reduction – An Indigenous Perspective." He writes:

At some point the Left in the so-called U.S. realized that convincing people to rally behind a "lesser evil" was a losing strategy. The term "harm reduction" was appropriated to reframe efforts to justify their participation and coerce others to engage in the theater of what is called "democracy" in the U.S. The idea of a ballot being capable of reducing the harm in a system rooted in colonial domination and exploitation, white supremacy, hetero-patriarchy, and capitalism is an extraordinary exaggeration. There is no person whose lives aren't impacted everyday by these systems of oppression, but instead of coded reformism and coercive "get out the vote" campaigns towards a "safer" form of settler colonialism, we're asking "what is the real and tragic harm and danger associated with perpetuating colonial power and what can be done to end it?" [...] And while the harm reduction sentiment may be sincere, even hard won marginal reforms gained through popular support can be just as easily reversed by the stroke of a politician's pen. If voting is the democratic participation in our own oppression, voting as harm reduction is a politic that keeps us at the mercy of our oppressors.

Additionally, like nonprofits, electoral politics in the United States cause further harm by co-opting movements and diverting energy and resources away from meaningful initiatives that tangibly empower communities.

During modern presidential election cycles, more than $10 BILLION(!) is regularly spent on campaign funding alone. According to the Federal Election Commission, Kamala Harris' failed 2024 presidential campaign spent a staggering $1.5 billion in just over three months, with much of those funds going towards celebrity concerts and influencer endorsements. A large portion of this money is donated by working-class Americans who believe in the democratic process, and are increasingly willing to donate to political candidates as societal conditions worsen.

There are also millions of volunteers contributing countless hours of labor to canvass, fundraise, campaign, engage in poll work, and rally for their political party or candidate of choice.

Many of these people are wholly invested in the electoral process and content in participating year after year, despite a lack of meaningful results. Some simply haven't been exposed to more effective modes of liberation that can easily be drowned out by the electoral chorus, or they reject any solution that could result in violence. They believe voting is the only option—or at least the safest one.

But if you look at virtually all of the lasting and significant progressive victories won throughout American history (and indeed human history), voting wasn't the catalyst. The catalyst was most always organized resistance or outright war. Elections won't save us because their primary purpose is to deter the masses from forcefully asserting our rights.

As community organizers, our paths will frequently cross with groups and individuals committed to political campaigns and electoral politics. There was a time when most radicals were equally invested in the illusion of electoral choice. Don't waste energy trying to debate or influence individuals into abandoning their devotion to politicians and reform, but make space for those who are ready to direct their energy and efforts elsewhere.

I'll leave you with additional insights from George Jackson's *Blood In My Eye*:

> We will not be distracted by such empty questions as who will be elected from which political party. All political parties, as things stand, will support the power complex. [...] What would help us, in fact, is to allow as many right-wing elements as possible to assume 'political' power. The warnings that 'our thrusts toward self-determination will bring on fascism' are irresponsible—or better, unrealistic. The fascists already have power! An electoral choice of ten different fascists is like choosing which way one wishes to die. The holder of so-called high public office is always merely an extension of the hated ruling corporate class. It is to our benefit that this person be openly hostile, despotic, unreasoning. [...] This is a huge nation dominated by the most reactionary and

violent ruling class in the history of the world, where the majority of the people simply cannot understand that they are existing on the misery and discomfort of the world. [...] We are faced with two choices: Continue as we have done for [a century], fanning our pamphlets against the hurricane, or build a new revolutionary culture that we will be able to turn on the old culture. Collectively we have that choice.

XVI

TRUTH IS...
THE PROBLEM WITH MEN

TW: Detailed descriptions of DV

~~~

When I was 3 years old, my father hit my mother so hard that he fractured her orbital bone. She was wearing glasses at the time, and the glass fragments penetrating her skin caused blood to shoot up and hit the ceiling. This is my earliest memory.

Incidents like this were a regular occurrence throughout my childhood. When my father left, another violent man would take his place. And another, and another, until I was in middle school. These attacks on my mother traumatized me. I'd often fall asleep to the sound of her screaming for help or sobbing from the next room. I can't recall one instance of a neighbor intervening, aside from a few calls to the police, who showed up and did nothing.

At first, I blamed my mother.

I thought if she'd just be quiet or do what she was told, she wouldn't get hurt. But as I got older, I realized these men were wantonly dangerous, and I began to blame myself for not doing more to stop them. My young mind thought that what made these men unsafe were their physically violent tendencies, so I worked hard to suppress those urges within myself. I promised that when I grew up I would be different—I'd challenge men who were abusive and simply walk away before ever raising my hands to a woman.

What I failed to realize, however, was that what actually made these men dangerous was their anger and insecurity, and their inability to regulate their emotions. And this glaring misjudgment led me to become exactly like them.

I stayed true to my promise to never raise my hands to a woman, but I found new ways to hurt those around me. I lashed out when I was angry because I couldn't manage my feelings or process my trauma, just like what I'd observed as a child. I internalized toxic behavior, and most of the men I encountered throughout my life were no different—scared boys who grew up to be dangerous men.

This is who I am today. There's not a resolution here where I tell you I did all the work necessary to change and become a healthy, non-toxic man. I read the relevant books and went to years of therapy in an attempt to improve myself, but those things mainly provided me with the introspection to understand who I was, not the capacity or aptitude to heal.

I remain a work in progress and continue to cause harm despite my best efforts. I have boundary issues that are no doubt exacerbated by my various social disorders, and my coping mechanisms are generally unhealthy and sporadic. When frustrated, I have been a cruel bully to friends, family members, and partners alike. I have made people uncomfortable with my crass attempts at humor. I have let my anger and impulsiveness lead me to make poor decisions that have caused people to get hurt. I am a criminal. I drink too much, I work too much, and I have pushed loved ones away out of fear and shame. Despite all of this, I'm frequently considered "one of the good ones," since patriarchy lowers the bar for all men.

I say this because I believe people have a right to see organizers for who we are, but also because our value as human beings isn't contingent on our faults or virtues.

There are no "good" or "bad" people because those binaries (like most binaries) are oversimplifications. Many organizers would agree, but organizational spaces remain filled with individuals hiding their true character for fear of being exposed or discarded. We think sanctity is the admission paid to align ourselves with freedom fighters and revolutionaries, so we cast ourselves in a false light, not realizing our shadows betray us.

Our standards for acceptable behavior are skewed by misrepresentation and the pressures to exhibit perfection and feign innocence above all else. But the fact remains that causing harm is inevitable, and those who think otherwise pose a unique threat to themselves and others.

The amount of harm cisgender men inflict on society, however, remains disproportionate, so their impact on movement spaces is often devastating. In fact, the mere presence of men in these spaces can be, at best, a distraction and, at worst, a detriment.

I challenge anyone to name a social movement that hasn't been significantly disrupted by the actions of harmful men engaged in liberation work.

Martin Luther King was exposed to be a notorious womanizer after his death. **Huey P. Newton** was accused of repeatedly raping fellow Black Panther leader Ericka Huggins. **JFK**, while holding office, allegedly impregnated a 15-year-old babysitter and had a lengthy affair with another teenage intern. **Frederick Douglass** had a white mistress for 28 years(!), who completed suicide when she found out Douglass had married yet another mistress shortly after his first wife's death. **Nelson Mandela** reportedly beat his first wife, Evelyn Mase, on several occasions and allegedly threatened to kill her with an ax. And **Mahatma Gandhi** called Black people "dirty animals" and slept naked with teenage girls to test his own celibacy. The list is seemingly endless, and the consequences have been exponential.

In addition to the direct harm imposed on victims, this type of flagrant behavior is a burden to those knowingly or unknowingly working with abusive men toward common socio-political goals. Collaborators are forced to choose between willfully ignoring the abuse, aiding in covering it up, attempting to expose the perpetrators, or abandoning their involvement on conscientious grounds. They may even be influenced into emulating patterns of harm being tolerated and enabled within their community.

Historically, harmful men are protected for fear of sullying the movement, but the outcome remains the same in terms of effort and energy expended to keep up appearances—and many organizations have collapsed from the ensuing chaos.

There's also the unfortunate consequence that sound political ideologies can be discredited by the actions of dangerous men serving as figureheads within social movements. When these men are inevitably exposed, the ideas they've promoted can be called into question by regressives seeking to undermine radical thought. But political ideologies are not akin to art created by abusive artists, since political ideologies are not crafted or upheld by any one individual.

In Arabic, there is a saying: "al haq hai haq," which suggests *the truth is the truth*, regardless of who speaks it. The existence of harmful men within radical movements doesn't automatically invalidate their beliefs just because they failed to live up to them. The truth is still the truth.

Nevertheless, the unchecked actions of men in organizing spaces can still be treacherous and discouraging to those seeking radical alternatives to dominant social and political systems, and impacted communities are left with few options to address this issue.

Anyone actively engaged in serious harm or abuse shouldn't be enabled or supported in movement spaces, unless it's to receive help to better themselves. As organizers, we need basic standards of decency for our own safety and the safety of the community. Voluntarily working with rapists, domestic abusers, or anyone posing a *clear* and *legitimate* danger to the community is not acceptable, and will only call your credibility into question.

That being said, removing harmful men from communities altogether—aside from being carceral and punitive—is generally not practical and only exacerbates the problem. And in rare instances where abusive men are unceremoniously removed from a given community, they often just go to another community and wreak havoc. Banishment is the "vote local" of accountability, and mainly serves to drive abuse further underground.

"We won't end the systemic patterns of harm by isolating and picking off individuals, just as we can't limit the communicative power of mycelium by plucking a single mushroom from the dirt," writes author and activist adrienne maree brown. "We need to flood the entire system with life-affirming principles and practices, to clear the channels between us of the toxicity of supremacy, to heal from the harms of a legacy of devaluing some lives and needs in order to indulge others."

A shift of that magnitude means making every effort to protect vulnerable people and spaces from predatory individuals seeking to cause harm. In doing so, we must also differentiate between harm (a negative impact resulting from an act or situation) and abuse (remorseless patterns of harmful behavior), and the varying levels of each when they occur.

We must prioritize impact over intent, while still taking both into account when warranted. And we must foster a culture of accountability that isn't applied selectively or in a biased, self-serving fashion. Patriarchy makes each of these undertakings all but impossible.

As a survivor and also a perpetrator of harm, I believe in the concepts of transformative and restorative justice. I have willingly participated in accountability processes in virtually every capacity, and seen them used in sincere terms and also misused as tools for revenge and deflection. Unfortunately, most communities don't yet have the infrastructure necessary to consistently implement trauma-informed processes for restorative justice that are accessible, fair, and steeped in "life-affirming principles."

Still, there are proactive and immediate steps men can take to reduce the prevalence of male harm in organizing spaces, and the impact that harm has on communities as a whole.

I'll outline some of those steps below in the hopes of providing men and boys a frame of reference to be better versions of ourselves while engaging in movement work. As always, these recommendations are not comprehensive and we should modify and adapt our approach as needed.

~~~

Listen to women

There's nothing I can ever add to this conversation that hasn't already been said by women and other marginalized genders for millennia; still, some things bear repeating. Women already hold the answers to much of our turmoil. For the sake of all humanity, it's imperative that men embrace the women in our lives and listen to them—even and especially if we disagree with what they may be saying.

The more likely a woman is to challenge men or call men out, the better. If you're a Black man, this doesn't necessarily apply to white women—who are prone to causing rampant harm themselves, in addition to racialized violence—but generally speaking, women have a better grasp on their emotions than men, and that's worth respecting and emulating.

Befriend women who don't have anything to offer you besides friendship. Interact with women you're not interested in sleeping with. Listen to your women partners and loved ones in earnest. Society has done a great job of denying men and especially boys the freedom to indulge in perspectives held by a full half of humanity. It's up to men to fix that.

De-escalate and walk away

I previously mentioned the value of men simply walking away when feeling provoked or lacking control in a tense situation. Too often, men insist on escalating situations by refusing to remove themselves. We are socialized in this manner, and institutions like the police have reinforced the notion that "backing down" is never an option. But removing ourselves is often the first method of stopping harm in its tracks, and its effectiveness can't be overstated. If you can't manage to control your emotions, simply walk away before you make things worse. And if there are vulnerable people who feel victimized by your mere presence, stay far away from them.

Take up less space

There are roles in the community that can not and should not be held by certain individuals—because their involvement would, at minimum, be a distraction and negatively impact the undertaking. For example, a white person shouldn't lead a lecture called "The Black Experience in America," because that would be weird and problematic. Similarly, when a man has caused egregious harm—such as sexual assault or domestic violence—their roles in the community may be severely and permanently limited, as they have forfeited certain privileges as a consequence of their behavior. How they addressed this behavior will factor in, but even complete repentance and transformation can't rewrite history.

Generally, men should already be taking up less space to allow for marginalized voices to be heard. So it's perfectly reasonable for men with a history of violence or abuse to take a backseat role as it pertains to certain aspects of community engagement.

There are plenty of opportunities to uplift and support movement work without perpetuating harm or triggering survivors. You don't have to go into hiding, but you don't have to lead every march, either.

Additionally, the less visible space you take up in movement work, the less likely you are to undermine that work with your actions or inactions. Sparingly engage in leadership roles, and never do so from a position of authority. Make decisions only as part of a group that prioritizes and amplifies the voices of women and other marginalized genders. Step back. Take breaks. Delegate and relinquish leadership duties and responsibilities.

This not only protects you from being a target to those in power, but also protects movement work from hinging on your behavior as an individual.

Channel your anger

Since male anger is dangerous and often deadly, refocusing that anger towards a deserving target can help mitigate harm. Instead of punching down towards people of marginalized genders, children, and those with less privilege; punch upwards towards cops, politicians, abusers, landlords, other men, and really anyone from the ruling class. In this context, "punch up" is both literal and a metaphor, since some men genuinely need to be beaten up. We can't stand by idly while abuse is happening. Self-defense is not always possible for victims, so as advocates, we need to keep our options open. Violence isn't usually the answer, but sometimes it is.

Anger can also fuel our other passions and interests. Learn a trade. Start an exercise regimen. Take up a pottery class. Write a book about community organizing while on the clock at work and then see if anyone will buy it. Get creative. Anger in itself is a valid emotion; it's what we do with that anger that renders it either harmful or helpful.

Do more housework and child-rearing

Women make up fewer than 10% of all gang members. That's because women don't have time to join gangs since they're too busy doing the majority of domestic labor. If you're a man trying to curtail harmful behavior, start by doing your share of the dishes and laundry. Pick up a mop without being asked. Cook a decent meal—and no, grilling hot dogs at a summer cookout doesn't count.

These are basic life skills that every adult should master, but for men, they have the added effect of keeping us out of trouble.

While you're at it, spend more time taking care of your children WITHOUT screaming at them or hitting them. This will help you learn empathy and patience, and even if it doesn't, at least you've done the bare minimum as a father. Win/win.

If you don't have your own children, you can still serve as a mentor or caregiver for children in need of adult influence and guidance. This can be done in a variety of ways, from spearheading a youth group to becoming a tutor or youth advocate. You can also help out women in your extended family who could probably also use a break from parenting as well.

As a general safety note: At no point should adult volunteers be alone with children who aren't in their direct care or custody. I'm a man who does a lot of community initiatives and events that center children, and I never find myself in situations where I'm alone with neighborhood kids in a private or unsupervised setting. It doesn't happen, and it doesn't need to happen. Even when coordinating child-themed events with free on-site childcare, we work in teams or in public and communal spaces. This is to help protect children from potential abuse. So, if you're keen on youth engagement, make sure you're doing so in a safe and conscientious manner.

Don't be a rapist

I can't stress this enough. Don't rape people.

Be accountable

Many people believe that accountability is something to be imposed on others who've done something perceived as harmful, but overwhelmingly accountability should center on *ourselves*. Instead of pointing fingers to absolve ourselves of wrongdoing, we should look internally for opportunities to improve. Surround yourself with people who are committed to healing and growth. Ditch abusive friends if they're unwilling to be decent human beings to others. Establish boundaries and moral expectations for those seeking access to your energy and time.

And remember that it's important to forgive yourself, regardless of whether or not others forgive you. Perpetual guilt and shame hinder our personal growth and serve no one. It's never too late to be the best version of yourself.

Be the person you needed as a child

Try as we may, it's unlikely that the Revolution will conclude during our lifetime. That means all liberation work—every protest, every meeting, every act of resistance—is ultimately being done for future generations. Now consider how far you've come since childhood, and what you could have accomplished if more adults in your life had your genuine best interest at heart... and then be that person for every child you encounter.

Being a beacon for children is its own reward, but it's also a sound investment towards transforming the future. The children we cultivate and empower today will be the freedom fighters of tomorrow. "It is easier to build strong children than to repair broken men," wrote Frederick Douglass, in between cheating on his wife. The truth is the truth.

When engaging with boys in particular, consider how caregivers and mentors can influence their behavior as they become men. Be intentional about holding male children to the same standards and expectations as girls. Correct boys when they emulate toxic behavior, and more importantly, model appropriate ways for them to engage in masculinity and boyhood. Coddling boys is not a substitute for love.

As noted by feminist scholar and author, bell hooks, "We don't really live in a culture that loves boys or loves children, and we don't encourage boys to be whole." Breaking that cycle is the first step in dismantling patriarchy. And we've gotta start somewhere.

EPILOGUE

In 1972, there was a plane crash in the Andes Mountains of South America. Forty-five people were on board, most of whom were young men and boys from a Uruguayan rugby team. About half of the passengers miraculously survived the crash.

The first night, however, temps plummeted to -40°F. More people died in the days following, as survivors waited for a rescue team that never came.

Those who did not succumb to their injuries or the frigid temps spent weeks on the mountain, with many resorting to cannibalism when starvation set in.

Sixteen men eventually made it home after successfully coordinating their own expedition down the frozen mountain to find help.

You may have seen a movie about this incident called *Alive*. There were also several books written by survivors.

The entire ordeal was astonishing.

But one detail about this event always stood out to me.

On the 11th day following the crash, some of the boys found a transistor radio that was still functioning.

While listening to a news broadcast, they were dismayed to learn that all search parties had been called off until Spring, as it was presumed there were no survivors from their flight.

The boys immediately descended into despair. They had no idea where they were, and hypothermia, malnutrition, and snow blindness were ravaging their bodies.

But one of the boys shouted, "Why are you crying? This is good news!"

The others grew angry with him and asked how he could say something like that after all they'd been through. The boy responded, "Now that we know nobody is coming, we're going to get out of here on our own."

He understood that without being shackled by the false hope of a rescue, they had an opportunity to reassess their circumstances and take matters into their own hands.

~~~

We're all on a mountaintop.

Society is collapsing around us. Things are markedly getting worse, and have been for decades. And we've waited for help.

We were told hard work would save us. But we've worked tirelessly and have less to show for it than our predecessors.

We were conditioned to think elections and laws would save us. But we've seen those same laws and policies get reversed when we needed them most. And we've seen progressively worse monsters rise to power.

We were programmed to think law enforcement and the military would save us. But they stand by idly at best, or bludgeon us to death at worst.

We were told selfless heroes would save us—the next Kennedy or Martin Luther King. But those men as we know them don't even exist. They have been romanticized, idolized, and propagandized to the point where they aren't real. There are no heroes coming.

And now that we know this, we have an opportunity to save ourselves.

Rather than descend into despair, we can act on this revelation and do what must be done.

We can organize and coordinate a plan.

We can empower ourselves and help one another.

We can accept the reality that even if all of us don't survive, many of us will. So we have a duty to live and die in solidarity with one another and prioritize the most vulnerable.

What a beautiful gift; to see the world in that way when faced with a foreboding truth.

Sixteen people on that mountain decided to save themselves, and they did.

And so will we.

ACKNOWLEDGMENTS

I would like to express my sincerest gratitude to the many people who supported and encouraged me throughout this creative process, and indeed for the past several years leading up to it. To my loving partners who never gave up on me and listened as I rambled about politics for months on end. To my children, who asked over and over, "But why are you writing a book?" forcing me to examine my motives every step of the way. To my mom, who won 3rd place in an Altamont Fair essay writing contest when she was 15 years old and saw fit to mount the plaque prominently in the house for me to stare at as a child. To my many editors, who gracefully and lovingly reminded me that I don't know anything about grammar; punctuation—or speling. To my talented and patient illustrator, who took me seriously when I said "OK, now draw a roach." To my good friend and photographer, who managed to capture my entire essence in one photo; and to her brother who somehow enhanced that imagery with a pencil and a sketchpad. To the countless folks who've asked me to write a book or run for office over the past decade—and to those who helped me make the right choice. To my comrades and contemporaries who've taught me so much and stood with me on the front lines of The Struggle. To the artists who inspire me. To the drug dealers who give me drugs. To U-Haul for always being there for me and never asking too many questions. And lastly, to the Freedom Fighters and Revolutionaries who came before me— thank you for your guidance and wisdom; and to those who will come after me—may your actions be bold and your convictions unwavering. The kids are depending on us. We bring wood to the fire.

ALTAMONT FAIR
1975
ESSAY CONTEST
3RD PLACE

REFERENCES

Arnove, Robert F., et al. (1982). *Philanthropy and Cultural Imperialism: The Foundations at Home and Abroad*

brown, adrienne maree (2020). *We Will Not Cancel Us: And Other Dreams of Transformative Justice*

Burke, Tarana (2021). *Unbound: My Story of Liberation and the Birth of the Me Too Movement*

Carson, Clayborne (1995). *In Struggle: SNCC and the Black Awakening of the 1960s*

Chávez, César, & Jenson, Richard (2002). *The Words of César Chávez*

DuBois, W.E.B. (1956). *I Won't Vote*

Fought, Leigh (2017). *Women in the World of Frederick Douglass*

Hampton, Fred (1969). *Power Anywhere Where There's People!*

Hoffman, Abbie (1974). *Steal This Book*

hooks, bell. (2011). *How Do You Practice Intersectionalism? An Interview with bell hooks by Randy Lowens* - Northeastern Anarchist #15

INCITE! Women of Color Against Violence (2017). *The Revolution Will Not Be Funded: Beyond the Non-Profit Industrial Complex*

Jackson, George L. (1972). *Blood in My Eye*

Le, Vu (2023). *We Need to Talk About Suicide Among Nonprofit Professionals and Social Justice Activists*

Lenin, Vladimir (1917). *The State and Revolution*

Lewis, Sinclair (1935). *It Can't Happen Here*

Morales, Iris (1996). *¡Palante, Siempre Palante! The Young Lords* (PBS)

Nechayev, Sergey (1869). *Catechism of a Revolutionist*

Oates, Stephen B. (2014). *The Fires of Jubilee: Nat Turner's Fierce Rebellion*

Preston, Ruby (2020). *Voting is Not Harm Reduction – An Indigenous Perspective*

Riley, Cole Arthur (2024). *Black Liturgies: Prayers, Poems and Meditations for Staying Human*

Shakur, Assata (1988). *Assata: An Autobiography*

Wagner, Sally Roesch (2001). *Sisters in Spirit: Haudenosaunee (Iroquois) Influence on Early American Feminists*

Wald, Karen (1971). *Remembering the Real Dragon: An Interview with George Jackson*

X, Malcolm, & Haley, Alex (1992). *The Autobiography of Malcolm X: As Told to Alex Haley*

www.ingramcontent.com/pod-product-compliance
Lightning Source LLC
Chambersburg PA
CBHW072345090426
42741CB00012B/2931